MW01609802

1440
Minutes Matter When Living An Intentional Life

Anthony Meyers

DEDICATION

This book is dedicated to the women in my life who have made me a better husband, father and son. To my wife Marilyn, my daughters Marshaye and Alexis, and my mother Barbara: you have all made me a better man.

I love you all very much.

CONTENTS

ACKNOWLEDGMENTS

To all those who said I couldn't, I wouldn't, and I shouldn't; I didn't listen. Every day that I was distraught, depressed, or despondent; I didn't give up. I found through turmoil, frustration, and times of loneliness that I must make every moment matter and cherish each.

To TD Jakes, Greg Holder and Earle Raveneau I must thank you for being transformative in my life. Each of you has taught me power and humility, forcefulness, and grace and how to be a better human being. I honor each of you by spending every day trying to make someone else's life more powerful, more productive, and more purposeful.

The journey continues..

CHAPTER 1

TIME WELL SPENT

*"That's one small step for man,
one giant leap for mankind."*

Neil Armstrong
American Astronaut

In my youth, a seemingly much simpler time, life was a world of amazement, fun, and adventure. Things like world dominance, corporate success, and the ticking clock meant little to me. That all changed with the words of the 35th President of the United States, John F. Kennedy. From behind a podium at Rice Stadium in Houston, Texas, Kennedy spoke of exceptionalism, hope, and time. A new age was dawning. Our collective future was bright. Kennedy said, "We choose to go to the moon in this decade and do other things, not because they are easy, but because they are hard."[1] I wasn't there when he spoke those defining words on September 21, 1962, but my clock was ticking.

The United States, through the National Aeronautical and Space Administration (NASA), was in a fierce race to be the first to set foot on the moon. This was more than a mere objective or scientific adventure; it was a true American obsession. Humanity, with childlike awe, has looked upon the stars and moon as some fantastic tapestry of mythical lore. Beautiful, but beyond the realm of attainment; impossible.

The best and brightest scientists, adventures, and daredevils were assembled and worked around the clock. Conventional wisdom and past theory were deemed relatively inefficient as cutting-edge technologies were explored and perfected to push the limits on what the human body could endure and technology could create. New technology and theory were put to the test as time raged on. Everything was put to the test because of the time.

NASA, with rooms filled with men in horned rimmed glasses and pocket protectors, pooled all of their collective resources and focused their efforts to make sure that their closest rival and international adversary, the Union of Soviet Socialist Republics (USSR), would not beat them to the ultimate destination, the moon. This was "the" race of all time. Every minute mattered. This was a race that would forever change the landscape of thought. It would define what a nation and a people, when pushing the limit, could and would ultimately accomplish.

However, there are inevitable bumps in the road, detours, unfortunate missteps, and even tragedies in every monumental endeavor. This would be no different. It was the case on January 27, 1967, when Apollo 1, with crew Virgil "Gus" Grissom, Edward H. White, II, and Roger B. Chaffee, had an epic and tragic failure that took the lives of all three as the command module was engulfed in fire.[2]

It was a heart-wrenching tragedy beyond measure. It is during tragic times like these that the doubters and dissenting voices often emerge. Many said this dream was too big, hope too high, and the cost too extreme. Maybe it was the opportunity to slow down or even stop. But to succeed, from the ashes of tragedy, you have to persist. Persistence must prevail. Finish! This was the race against time to define a generation and change generations to come.

With all their eggs in one very expensive basket, the US did what others said was impossible, when on July 16, 1969, Apollo 11 blasted off from the Kennedy Space Center in Florida.

"That's one small step for man, one giant leap for mankind."

Neil Armstrong

Her crew, the best of the rest, were Michael Collins, Edwin "Buzz" Aldrin, Jr., and Neil Armstrong. They were the hope of their generation. At that moment, time and opportunity would intersect. In just six breathtaking days, and with great expectation, Apollo 11 landed on the Moon. Moments later, with the world and our adversaries watching, American Neil Armstrong stepped out of his lunar landing module, the Sea of Tranquility, and became the first to step on the Moon. We made it first. The date was July 20, 1969 at 10:56 p.m. EDT[3]; I was six.

It seems funny now to delve into the history of it all. This dynamic competition of wit and wisdom was, in simplistic terms, for bragging rights. To say, "We did it first." In reality, the battle was not against each other, our adversaries, or the final destination. In the quest for the galactic Holy Grail, what was consistently fought, was time. The actual final frontier is the all-elusive commodity of time. Time is the one thing to which all of us has an equal claim. It is the ultimate unifier. Whether you are rich or poor, intelligent or illiterate, cute or as ugly as four o'clock in the morning, we each get the same amount of time. And time doesn't care; it's emotionless.

There are 1440 minutes in each day, no more, no less. You have each minute to use with wisdom and grace or to squander asleep at the wheel of your destiny's drive. Time is the currency that cannot be redeemed and only has future value. Then, how is it that one person can wake up in the morning (on time), press forward toward perfection and promise, meet and exceed their daily goals, and end the day with a sense of accomplishment; all the while, another will sleep the day away, wake up, stretch and continually wonder "where did the day go?"

Rich or poor, the in-crowd or outcast, racially or sexually undefined, we all have the same 1440. Minutes cannot be borrowed, bought, stolen, nor stored. They are merely used or abused. The choice is ultimately and solely yours. The accurate measure of success is how those precious minutes are spent.

Let's paint a picture of your day. First, let's account for sleep, so dedicate six hours for that (no, not eight hours; remember, you are trying to reach your goal. Sleep gets sacrificed.) That adds up to 360 minutes. Now, allow 8 hours for work; that's 480 minutes. This leaves you 600 minutes. I am sure it seems like a lot, but like a vapor, it will vanish in an instant as if it were never there. Bathroom breaks, eating, moving from point A to B will take another mindless 3 hours or 180 minutes. Now you have 220 minutes to ensure your daily dreams come true.

The beginning of your day is typically where all the trouble begins. This is when excuses become time killers and dream diverters. Have you found yourself saying, "I'm tired, I can catch up tomorrow" or "I don't have enough time to finish what I have to do." Let's be honest. There are no excuses for not making the best of every day. As an anonymous writer once wrote, "Excuses are the tool of incompetence, they build a monument of nothing, and those that specialize in them are seldom good for anything but excuses, excuses, excuses." I heard this as a child and have spoken and lived by this creed for years.

Think about this:

To realize the value of ONE YEAR, ask a student who failed a grade.

To realize the value of ONE MONTH, ask a mother who gave birth to a premature baby.

To realize the value of ONE WEEK, ask the editor of a weekly newspaper.

To realize the value of ONE HOUR, ask the parents to wait outside their sick child's operating room.

To realize the value of ONE MINUTE, ask a person who missed their flight.

To realize the value of ONE SECOND, ask a person who just avoided an accident.

To realize the value of ONE MILLISECOND, ask the person who won a silver medal instead of gold.[4]

All of us want to control time to meet our needs and expectations. The family members visiting with a loved one who is about to pass away wish they could have more time. The individual waiting for the doctor to call with test results wishes time would move more swiftly. To a greater degree are the scores of people who would reverse or redeem the time to start life over if given the opportunity. They wish they could press reset and go back to a particular point in time.

Here is a reality check. Life isn't fair, and there is no video game-like reset button to start over as if nothing happened. That said, and since you can't redeem the time, you must take control and full advantage of every minute.

The 1440 minutes of equal access must be maximized to build and sustain a successful life.

CHAPTER 2

TIME KEEPS ON TICKING

"Show me a guy who's afraid to look bad, and I'll show you a guy you can beat every time."

Lou Brock
Major League Baseball Hall of Famer
(St. Louis Cardinals)

When all you have is your reputation, your "word," it must stand for something. Respect in your business or personal life demands that you be a person of action. Positive and corrective action for which you can be counted on. It should be that if you say it, it happens, and people can count on it. Being on time is exactly that, being where you said you would be when you said you would be there - not just showing up, but well prepared and on time.

Over time and in a shifting business community, we have allowed society to dictate time, where late is the norm rather than the exception. It even has a name, "fashionably late." What is that? Late is late. In fact, on time is often too late. But there seems to be some glory or satisfaction from having to make people wait. I call it the arrogance of importance. Some of us can get to be so important, with some delusions of grandeur, that we even disrespect time itself.

Our heightened sense of self-importance drives us to double-book appointments and reschedule meetings as we hold other people's time in our hands. Being consistently late diminishes the level of deference you have, regardless of the position you hold. That lack of respect evolves into indifference for all you represent because you can't keep their word.

It most often reflects in people who come to work late, discernibly every day. As if the next day was a surprise, somehow in their mind they did not see it coming, they prepare to be late and then rushed to make time work in their favor. Meetings, reports, and assignments are continually late, and to explain it all, they offer some poorly crafted excuse of how there was not enough time to get it all done. Time itself was the culprit to their demise. This never works, but they try, nonetheless.

The only way to break this pattern is to get ready for tomorrow, yesterday. You may gain success by not keeping your word, but small things consistently add up to a compounded effect. Being on time is too late. Let's establish that on time means fully prepared for excellence. If excellence is not the norm, being on time doesn't matter. You need to be early. Sustainable success is gained by those that can manage and maximize their time.

Prioritize Your Time – Defining Success

What or who is truly important to you, and how do you spend time in that area? What is the priority you place on things? What is your priority for life? Is it money, family, fame, health, power, title, position or something else? Regardless of what it is, there is a value, conscious or not, placed upon it. You have developed some sort of matrix, knowingly or not, to assign a point scale, if you will, to everything important to you. Since every minute counts, it's important to take a look at the value you assign t your minutes so you can begin to stop wasting time.

Which is more valuable to you, dinner with a friend or with a high-profile client? Do you prioritize going back to school for that MBA or work harder and position yourself for advancement? Both are quite time-consuming but rarely done effectively simultaneously. Therefore, one becomes the priority over the other. The question that you must ask is, "Where do I want to end up, and what am I willing to sacrifice to get there?" That is the definitive question you must answer.

Make no mistake about it; there will be sacrifices to get time under control. Everyone or everything is not worthy of your time or attention, nor should it be. When you decide what or who will have your attention, you will invariably leave someone or something out. But, they are abandoned for a more significant cause. I know that abandoned may seem like a harsh word, but you can't be in two places at once. The ultimate goals and objectives you set for yourself are your main focus. How you allot your time should align with your priorities. If not, your goals will not be met. Your time will ultimately be wasted.

One of your most difficult decisions will be defining how to stop the outflow or misuse of your time. Begin by doing the one thing that is the most difficult for most of us; saying the word "no." That's right, the word "no" begins the process of prioritization. It says that you don't have time for certain things and are willing to sacrifice to find the time. Whenever your time is required, determine if it helps accomplish your goals for any given day. If not, say "no." If the dinner with a friend rather than a client is the true priority, bump the client. If not, bump the friend. How about people that waste time with mindless emails, phone calls, Facebook, Zoom, TikTok, and Twitter? Let them know that you don't have time to talk, twiddle your thumbs, or answer to them at this time.

I have a friend who is a doctor and a highly sought-after speaker. Her time is always at a premium. If you have the good fortune to have her cell phone number, you will have the misfortune to find that she does not answer your call, and you need to leave her a message. Her message says, "I am sorry that I am unavailable to accept your call at this time, so you may want to call back later since I will not check the messages left on this phone. Thanks, and have a great day." It seems somewhat harsh, but she doesn't have, nor does she take the time, to offset her day and waste minutes. Thus, no priority is placed on dealing with phone messages until it is their time. Though I thought it was bazaar and ineffective, I now see that her life continues to display focus and sustainable success. The time spent answering messages was leveraged more effectively to respond to emails and only those that fit into the goals for the day.

What are you willing to put on your priority list? More importantly, what and whom are you ready to get rid of or put on the sideline? These questions need to be answered every day. For starters, take the opportunity to look through your cell phone. How many contacts do you have that are useless?

I was updating my phone one day, and it was taking entirely too long, and I wondered why. Then I noticed that it had to load more than 800 contacts. Wow, more than 800; I must be a popular dude. That was not necessarily the case. Some were people that I lost touch with or didn't even remember meeting. Then there were some whom I knew I would never talk to and others with disconnected numbers. As I looked further, I found a core group—family, friends, mentors, advisors, mentees, and business associates— people with whom I am in constant relationship. These are the individuals that have a hand in the direction of my life. They are the ones that I place a priority on and allow my time to be spent well with them.

You must seek ways to prioritize time for those who matter and keeps you on your path toward success. If you are serious about attaining daily success, you have to make time for the things and people that matter. I cut my contact list by almost half and redefined my focus on daily sustainable success.

Keep a Calendar

Whether you like it or not, our lives are dictated by the calendar. You use it to look at your past and plan your future: the annual round of work, meetings, appointments, holidays, birthdays, and other events in life. How many times have you missed one of them?

The date of our birth, personal milestones, and failures finds their way onto that same calendar. Each event, public or personal, great or small, has a day, month, and year that fixes its place in time. Since everything fits within the realm of what needs to be placed on a calendar, you would be wise to put yourself in line with it.

Begin to schedule everything every day. Put it all on a calendar. Yes, write it down. Time to wake, eat and sleep. Every meeting, every appointment, project, and deadline. Leave nothing to chance—schedule brief gaps between meetings to rejuvenate or just to use the restroom. Trust me, nobody is going to give you the time, so you must take it. I have an Apple Watch that has an app that tells me I need to breathe. Just 60-seconds to slow down and breathe. There are times that the app will notify me it is time to breathe for 60-seconds. Just slowly breathe in and out for one minute. At first, my response to it was to dismiss it because "I don't have time to breathe right now." Silly as it may seem, that is how I thought of it. Not anymore. Breathing is kind of essential, so I don't dismiss the opportunity to slow down and breathe. Whether I'm in a meeting, driving, eating dinner, or whatever. I don't dismiss the essential. Intentional breathing is now part of my schedule—drive time to and from work, watching TV, or surfing social media while answering emails—you will find me focused on breathing.

When you look at your calendar, what you begin to notice is how your time is spent and with whom. You begin to see things that are beneficial and things that are not. And, when you see those unnecessary things, it makes it easier for you to want to fix or change them. You can then make your calendar the path by which you follow - to the letter. All items that don't fit into your calendar are now determined to be a non-priority and you can say "no" to them by not adding them.

Know When to Sacrifice Time

There is always a battle raging for your time. No matter what you do, you can't control or manipulate time. It is a constant that never slows. You must learn to use it as a tool and take full advantage of it. You also must discern how to manage competing interests for your time as you can't be in two places at once.

Scanning through the endless channel offering on TV, I once saw on an old Ed Sullivan show about a man that spun plates on the end of a stick. He would spin and balance a plate then move onto another. One after another he would spin plate after plate. As he got to the end of the row of plates, 12 stood spinning. It seemed quite masterful. He stood there with a brief gleam in his eye, but without time to bask in the glory of his accomplishment, he ran back to the first plate and began spinning again.

One after another he spun plates. If he was too slow getting to any plate, it stood the fate of falling to the floor and crashing in irreversible failure. Back and forth he ran, but with all of his skill and strategic planning, plates fell. As I looked on, I realized that I was running my life the same way. I was trying to juggle too many things at one time, desperately trying not to drop anything. I felt, rather than plates, they were chainsaws poised for my imminent demise.

Many of you are doing the same thing. Panic races through your mind, and questions begin to echo through each waking hour, maybe even in your dreams such as, "What will happen if I drop something?" or "Who will be affected?" or "What will I lose?" and quite possibly, "Who is going to know?" Your level of anxiety increases as doom and gloom consumes your every thought. But, you must STOP THE MADNESS!

Here is where the sacrifice of time comes in. You have to remember that there is only so much time available to focus on the most important "plates" in your life. So, what then do you do with the rest? How do you determine which ones are your priority? Maybe you can choose to spin some plates less, but you may not maximize your potential. If some plates fall, you may choose to hide the pieces. Which plates do you let fall, and which do you keep spinning?

The reality is some of these plates aren't your responsibility. Return them to whomever they belong. Also, there are some plates you just can't or shouldn't keep spinning. It's ok to set those down.

For those plates that are truly yours and are pertinent to the direction you are going, spend your time learning how to become a more proficient spinner with them. And, learn how to keep them spinning at a pace that you can handle. You will always be tempted to accept new plates as opportunities arise, but you need to recognize that if you accept another plate, you may jeopardize all that you already have. And, some plates will inevitability crash if you don't recognize your limits.

Though you may be the one who put most of the plates in your life into motion, you may realize that you can no longer keep them all spinning. This is where priorities come in. For you to keep your family, finances, career goals all spinning, you must say "no" to others that stand in the way. If you take on anything else, it is at the expense of allowing what is spinning to wobble and fall.

Life is truly a balancing act. It is when you keep adding and subtracting without reason or regard to the situation, you end up imbalanced, and consequently, with a life filled with chaos. Even when you have established a prioritized set of goals, things can sometimes feel overwhelming and on the verge of collapse. The better you are at assessing the value of adding anything else to your life, the more able you will be to keep all things in order.

Understand the Time Principle (Investment of Time)

Investment is a term related to saving or deferring consumption. The term has several closely-related meanings in business management, finance, and economics. Most say that an investment is an asset that is usually purchased, or equivalently a deposit is made in a financial institution in hopes of getting a future return or interest. The word originates from the Latin "vestis," meaning garment, and refers to the act of putting things (e.g., money or other claims to resources) into others' pockets.[5] Like everyone, you want to invest and reap a huge return. The assumption is that if you invest wisely, there will be a return that will meet your future needs.

Perhaps the most difficult questions any investor has to ask are "Where do I invest?" or "What is my risk?" or even "What is my rate of return?" All are difficult questions to be answered and are all bound by time. But, to receive the ultimate return on your investment, it is wise to invest in yourself. This means that you have to take time to improve yourself socially, economically, emotionally, physically, and spiritually. That's right. TAKE the time; nobody is going to give it to you.

If you want that promotion and an MBA is what is required, then take the time to go back to school. Day, night, online classes; it doesn't matter, but get it done NOW! Been to law school, but after several attempts, have you failed to pass the Bar Exam? Well, now is the time—you take it again and again. There is no excuse for your failure of self-investment. Failure is a learning opportunity that allows you to grow if you have the proper mindset. Read a book, attend seminars, listen to a podcast, or sit at the feet of a great mentor.

Do whatever it takes to make your dream come true, but know that this will take a committed time investment. If you decide to go back to school, you will need time for class, studying, and class cohorts and projects. You will also have to cut back on time for friends, fun, and sleep.

While, you might be afraid of the unknown, failing or what the future brings, you have to take risks to get to reach your goals and ultimately the pinnacle of success. It may not be easy, but try to use any failures as motivation to take your next step. Reassess your time and focus on the goal forward. Never stop moving forward.

The Value of Your Time (Quality of Time)

What is your value? Do you know what you are worth? How much is your time worth? An attorney has little problem letting you know their worth. They call them billable hours. They assess a value for the time to deal with other people's problems. Whether it's $200 or $1,000 per hour, they have no hesitation in letting you know their time is essential. Your financial investment gives you access to their time.

If you can't put an amount on the value of your time, then you will allow others to use up some of the vital seconds you have each day. Your 1440 will mean absolutely nothing. Since you have such little time to spare, then you must assess how to take a stand on your time. Ensure that if your time is spent, something productive and positive comes of it.

Stop allowing the agendas of others to dictate your time or derail you from your path. I am sure you have a shortlist of people that you see as time killers. These people are called Drainers. Drainers are just as their title depicts. They drain you emotionally and physically. They suck the life out of you and your dreams. They come to each encounter with their agenda, pushing you and your plans to fit their plan and pace. They often want you to solve their problem or take their side in whatever their agenda is. They can use any opportunity with you to whine and complain about an array of things and the unfairness of their life.

It the Drainer's nature to take as much as they can from you while leaving you wondering, "How did I get here, and how can I get away from them?" I recognize it sounds somewhat harsh, but you end up trying to hide from them by shielding yourself from emails, phone calls, meetings, texts, and any other form of communication, which translates to delegating it to others or relegating it to a non-response.

Drainers often arrive with their wheelbarrow of assorted daily distractions and dilemmas. You must be determined not to take what they drop at your feet and accept it as your own. You may have to deal with what they present you, but that doesn't mean any of it is yours. Don't get wrapped up in their emotions to such a level that you become emotionally invested in their problems.

The unfortunate part of this is that Drainers are, more often than not, the closest people in your life. They tend to be family and friends who are much harder to dismiss or ignore. But, now is the time to hash out a plan to redirect their direction. Position them toward your strength and make their time work for you. If not, you will find that the time spent with them are minutes thrown into the sea, never to be recovered. Set parameters on how, when, and where you will deal with each encounter. It must be on your terms, or you must have a more significant impact on how things will be directed.

It is easy at this point to have the image of a Drainer's face etched into your brain now, but don't. For most of your encounters with a Drainer, it is not a personal attack but just how they are wired and go through life. Now don't get me wrong. There are times that you will give all available moments to those around you who are in crisis, even if they drain you. But when a crisis becomes a regular event and not the exception but the norm, there is a problem. If people are consistently bringing you their trash, it's time to take a step back and reassess. You are not their trashcan, nor do you have the time to be.

Remember that Drainers are coming to drain; that's what they do. Don't look to them to be anything different. They are consistent. You know that dogs bark, and you probably have become accustomed to it and therefore expect it. There is never a time that I look at any dog and expect it to purr like a cat. That has never been my experience. Drainers are similar. They do what they do best, and you should expect and plan for it. A well-timed plan affords you the opportunity to enter into a conversation, deal with their issue and leave with minimal loss of self.

Fillers, on the other hand, are always ready to add something to your life. They bring words of encouragement and a positive direction. Each encounter is an experience that brings fulfillment and pushes you toward your goal. Those that fall into the category of "fillers" don't leave you with the baggage of unwarranted dramas or feeling worse off than when they entered your day. You may benefit from a Filler during a 3-minute hallway conversation or a 2-hour in-depth lunch. They always have gifting words of wisdom and cast a guiding light on a path to make your future look brighter. They have the ability to connect the dots on your course and can be the GPS guide to your success.

Always be looking for ways to allow Fillers into your life. There are times that you may be so self-consumed that you don't want to let anyone in, even if they are there to help. You must overcome that fear, recognize who the Fillers are in your life and give them space and time to add to your journey. However, this is not a one-sided relationship. You will have to bring a heightened sense of engagement, confidence, and the ability to ask good questions if you are to get the best out of these encounters. You should use your time spent with Fillers to attain wisdom, build a life that fosters better relationships.

Fillers and Drainers both access your life by the choices you make, the people that you align yourself with, and how you allot time on a daily basis. It's important to recognize each type in your life. You can almost always tell the type of person someone is by listening to them, watching the expressions on their face and the tone in their voice, text, or email.

Fillers and Drainers can have a dramatic role in how you act, react or respond in encounters with each. How you balance each of these types of people on a daily basis is critical. Make it a daily goal to be around more Fillers than Drainers. While you can't always control how many of each you are around, the power you have in the encounter is how you allow each to affect your day. For example, if you spend enough time with Fillers, it makes your interaction with

Drainers easier to navigate. The balance is to have Fillers consume much more of the available time you have than those that drain. Be careful not to let what was given by a Filler (words of wisdom, hope, guidance) be drained at such a rate that would leave you empty and in desperate need of filling. If you stay in an unbalanced state of giving away what you acquired, you may begin to take on the attributes of a Drainer.

ANTHONY MEYERS

CHAPTER 3

THE DAY KILLERS

"Out of clutter, find Simplicity. From discord, find Harmony. In the middle of difficulty lies Opportunity."

Albert Einstein
Scientist

You now have your calendar with your daily plans in hand and are focused on the purpose for the day. You can visualize your plan in its entirety, and all the provisions for the vision seem to be in place. This is your moment. Finally, your season has come. You awake in the morning with great anticipation of what the day will bring and the dynamic possibilities of getting closer to your dream. It's Monday! Just at that precise moment, the reality of the day comes into view. Trying to accomplish anything of significant value will always create obstacles that you will have to acknowledge and deal with. If you are going to get past the anticipation of the day to live out the day, you must take the time and be bold enough to fight forward.

When I was about twelve or thirteen, we lived in Raleigh, North Carolina. In a reasonably well-established neighborhood with all the trappings of middle-class success. When you are that age, the reality of life can oftentimes be true as a fantasy or as horrible as a bad dream. You realize that there is very little that you can control and must consistently process all the things that are happening to and around you. In this neighborhood, my neighborhood, there was a corner house about a block away that I would have to travel past to get to the park.

Even though the community was nice, this house seemed ominous. No particular reason; it just felt strange. The one thing that stood out, behind this long green chain-link fence, was a big, hairy, dirty dog. No discernable breed, just a big, hairy, dirty dog. He had a deep and vicious howling bark that made his presence all the more fierce. Most days, he would bark, growl and roam the fence line. Something that you would never get used to. He was very intimidating, and seemingly, if he had the opportunity, he would just sink his teeth into me. Occasionally, I would not go to the park for fear of this dog. This went on for a few months until I was informed that the family moved away and took their Big, Hairy, Nasty, Dog with them. I felt like a fool. I was not enjoying life for fear of something that was no longer there. It taught me a precious lesson at a young age. Never let the obstacles, perceived or actual, deprive you of enjoying life.

Emotional highs and lows can be overwhelming at times. Never be too ashamed or fearful to seek professional help. Don't do this alone. Help is available to you. Reach out and talk if you need it. That is a measure of leadership and success as well.

I am a strong advocate for counseling and have included these numbers as resources.

National Suicide Hotline - 1-800-273-8255

SAMHSA Treatment Referral Helpline - 1-877-726-4727

Your Family of Issues

Each of you has or will experience obstacles standing in our path that could divert you from attaining the goals you have set forth. Look at it this way. The "family" at your corner house is a bully named Self, his cousin, Past Issues, accompanied by his little sister, Insecurities. Aunt and Uncle, Fear and Anxiety, rock on the porch, and Grandma Doubt stands at the screen door with a discerning eye.

You may laugh at the assembly of this "family," but they are all too real of a threat, and they don't live around the corner or in the old neighborhood. Each of them knows that you don't want to walk their way or have any type of encounter with them. You will do almost anything not to cross their path. Yes, there are other ways around, but this is your path, your opportunity, and you shouldn't let anyone or anything stand in your way. Giving up is not an option. They mark residency in our thoughts and memories. There is no way to sidestep them. You must deal with them head-on each day.

Once you have learned to conquer, or at a minimum, control them, everything else is doable. You need to take a serious look at each member of this disturbed, dysfunctional, demoralizing, and demeaning family. If you can first understand their attributes, then possibly, you can develop a plan of attack and a mentality to deal with them. The goal is to overcome them individually and collectively. You can't let them win.

Bully - Self

Self is the first bully you must deal with and conquer

to get anything of purpose accomplished. This bully CAN be beaten, but you have to be prepared for the fight of your life. You were purposely crafted just as you are. Begin to trust who you are, not the finely curated individual you present to others.

Remember, you are uniquely designed and the only you there is. Acknowledge who you are and accept who you are becoming. It doesn't matter what you wear, how you style your hair (if you still have some), what imperfections you may get nipped or tucked, you are still going to be you. No matter where you go, there you are. You can't run from yourself. If you don't like who you are, change what you can. If you don't like who you have been, forgive yourself, then take steps to change for the better.

In your attempts to change, you may try to pattern yourself after someone else and end up becoming a lesser you. And, you will most likely spend most of your time trying to live up to the image of this phony person and have to compromise part of your own uniqueness to fit that mold. With each compromise, the best part of you is gets lost and often forgotten. Awaken your inner purpose for your best days, no matter your age, are yet to come. Applaud yourself for your uniqueness and begin to show on the outside the leader hidden on the inside. You weren't meant to be like everyone else, so be happy with the "you" in you. You are the baddest you there is. Be You. Be Confident. Be Great!

Cousin - Past Issues

One of the greatest tools you possess is your mind. It has the dexterity to store, organize and recall an array of commands from your memory. This multi-faceted, high-speed, natural computer can file away millions of events, thoughts, sights, sounds, scents, experiences, ideas, successes, and failures, all as you walk, talk, and sleep. It never shuts off.

Your memory is excellent when you can access what you want, when you want it, and can be convoluted when you can't remember where you left your keys. But, there are some memories that you want to dispose of that are forever etched in your mind. Undeletable. It is that blown business deal from five years ago that tore at your reputation. That argument with a loved one when you said something that "I'm sorry" didn't fix. It's the culmination of all the mistakes, missteps, and public successes and failures that you would like to hide and forget. They can plague your memories and mascaraed as your present truth.

These are the past issues that bring you so much pain. They can make you weary of trying something new or even trying over after past stumbles. Even if you get a handle on the memory, you must turn a deaf ear to the comments of others that would want to paint your past as a present-day portrait. There will always be someone who continues to bring up your history as a marker in time; stagnant. They will try to hold you in that same position as if you were still stuck in that same spot. Just because you may have missed the deadline and lost a big business deal in the past doesn't make you an incapable professional now.

It's time to deal with Cousin-Past Issues and repurpose your time to learn from past missteps and grow toward being better. Never allow yourself to get stuck in the past as if it is your final destination. The past is truly the past; leave it there. You are what your future says, not what your history holds. Move Forward.

Little Sister - Insecurities

Let's first look at this issue from the opposite direction—security. Security gives you a sense of protection against your fears. It is that mindset that guards and prevents damage or loss of all that you have. The peace gained by being in a secure environment or attitude allows for a more harmonious way of life. It would be great if you could live in a mindset of total security. Almost like the security children have when they jump into the arms of a waiting parent. There is no fear or anxiety, just the joy of the moment and experience; security.

Most of you have, at some pivotal times in your lives, dealt with thoughts, feelings, and the characteristics of insecurity. It is when your security is disrupted or broken that you feel a loss of control and stability. This is more than just a passing whim of emotion, but given root, it can derail the best and brightest of individuals. It can make you hesitate when a situation requires swift decisions or desert the obligation of responsibility when times get rough. It can even progress to the point where you find yourself hiding in the shadows of life, hoping everything will get better or just pass over.

When I was younger, I had the most challenging time speaking in front of groups. If I had to read something, I would stammer and stutter my way through. I felt so far outside of what I consider comfortable that I would dread any opportunity that had to do with speaking publicly. But, the opportunities kept coming. Nonetheless, I had to deal with my insecurity of wondering what people thought of me or if I would fail. I would tell myself, "I'm the best ME there is, and you can't beat me at being me. So, all I have to do is be ME." It began to work and still does. Although, I have to focus on making it work, so will you.

You can and must fight past all the thoughts and become secure in an insecure setting. Time is not the friend of insecurity. It always moves too fast. You don't have the luxury of wasting time being insecure about who you are or what you have to do. Time is consumed by not only the moment of an event but all the days, weeks, and months leading up to it.

Take a deep breath and take the next step. It may sound simplistic, but to take a step that you have found to be unstable in the past is a huge undertaking. But it is a step you have to take, nonetheless. You may even get sick to your stomach with the unsettling moments and days that life may bring, but you must remember that better times are coming. You can, should, and will have victory over the bad days. If you persist and persist you must. Ultimately, there will be times when life will give you situations that seem insurmountable, making it easy to retreat to some place of safety. In that false sense of security, you will be off track and away from your goal. Press on and get the job done. You can't reverse time, but you can create new positive experiences that can become the foundation of your security and give you the chance to wave goodbye to your sister, Insecurity.

Aunt - Fear

You must learn to take a calculated risk and not give in to Aunt Fear. I have found that the emotion of fear can be a lifesaver or a dream killer. It is that fight or flight emotion that can move in swiftly. It can motivate a parent to go into a burning house to save a child or freeze and stare with despair as the home is engulfed with flames. What can set you apart is how well you deal with the fears you face.

Each of you has some sort of fear, some mild and manageable, others that can be utterly unrealistic and become something that gets you out of our comfort zone on the verge of panic and irrational actions. You may have a fear of failing, rejection, poverty, disrupted life, or other people. Even the fear of success may cause some of you to alter your path of life drastically. Some of you can become so fearful of making any significant decision, or tell others how you feel, or even be truthful with yourself.

I have encountered many individuals who were highly qualified for a job or promotion, but they began to talk themselves out of applying out of a fear of rejection. They would often say something like, "I know I won't get the job," or "I don't have what they are looking for," or even "I'm not their type." Even if they would get the interview, they found themselves entering with a self-defeated demeanor and a fatalistic attitude. They added to that a blame game, holding others accountable for their own demise. Those thought patterns have a way of becoming a self-fulfilling prophecy or self-sabotage.

There is no way to succeed if you plan to fail. If you do, failure becomes an expectation and not the exception. Here's a thought, what if you made all your plans for success without the option of failure? No Plan B. No contingency plan nor safety net. All in.

I don't ride my motorcycle with training wheels in the backyard. I ride on the street with the reasonable expectation that I will not fall or get into an accident. I'm cautious but not afraid. The opposite of fear is risk. So, what are you willing to risk in accomplishing your goals? The risk is following an entrepreneurial pursuit while not submitting to the fear of failure and the seeming stability of an ordinary job. You must take the calculated, very intentional risk and not fear. It doesn't mean a mindless pursuit, but it is pushing past being struck with fear. You can't let your fear become so unrealistic that it consumes your life.

I had a classmate so afraid of spiders that when there was one in their car, they became irrationally distracted and ran off the road and wrecked the car. Yes, a disaster from the fear of a little spider. The car was damaged, but they were not. Was the fear equal to the panic or the ultimate result? Control the fear, respond appropriately, and Push On.

Uncle - Anxiety

It's that uncomfortable feeling that you get right before a big speech or as you await the final decision after a sales presentation. You are nervous, tense, frustrated, and entirely not yourself. Not just sweaty palms, but your whole body is in flux. The anxiety is so apparent that you can find it challenging to focus, speak or think properly. If you are honest, these feelings hit you at some point or another. Sometimes it may be easier to push past and overcome than others. But in order to be successful, it cannot be allowed to stop you.

I must confess that there are a select few things that still bring me an uncomfortable level of anxiety. Though I find it quite comfortable speaking in front of large groups, it can be a daunting task to speak in a room with five or ten. For me, in front of thousands, there is freedom and security that is lost in a small crowd. I say the same things, but feel differently about it.

I have had to conquer this by focusing on each task as a building block for success. Each block is my responsibility. Some are more manageable blocks for me than others, and it's easy to put those in place. Easy blocks are the things that I like to do and can be put in place with relative ease, and most often can be taken for granted. The harder blocks, like my speaking with a small group—and for you whichever blocks bring you the most anxiety—these challenging blocks give us the opportunity to become stronger.

I believe that every challenge is an opportunity to learn and grow. It is a type of weight training. Each time you face the swell of emotions that stems from any situation that brings anxiety, you should become a little more confident that you can get through it. You know that you can have a victory over it. They say, "It may not look pretty, but a win is still a win." I agree. Celebrate the small wins.

Some of what you do may be great and you may look graceful being incredible. You know the things that are easy, and you can do them with your eyes closed. The other things are harder and make you work and focus to be better at them. These things can make you anxious. Anxiety makes you appreciate what happens behind the scenes, it can allow you to be a better professional, leader, parent, or whatever your daily success is. Anxiety, within reason, can keep you sharp and very well aware that you are not perfect and that the kinks in our armor are just outward signs of maturity in the growth process of success.

You can't rush life, nor success. You have to plan for it and be prepared to carry the weight of it. You can't move Wednesday and replace it with Saturday because the situation doesn't fit or you are stressed about what is coming. Focus on the inevitable and recognize that tomorrow is coming precisely as yesterday did. You can't change it, but you do get to determine how you will think about and respond.

You should not be anxious about anything beyond the situation at hand or the area you influence. Time and opportunity will always cross paths. You must be well prepared to recognize and then take full advantage of each opportunity that comes your way. Many of you are very anxious about what is going to happen next at some particular point in time. Have you ever waited for the phone to ring after a job interview or for the subsequent text after a date? That waiting can bring unreasonable anxiety. Take control of the moments that you have each day, and don't look back. If the call comes, it comes; if not, move on to the next mountain and climb it. Time is ticking.

Grandma - Doubt

What are all the ways that you can talk yourself out of

doing something? There are always questions that give you pause in your decision-making process. Sometimes that pause allows you to gain a helpful perspective or purposeful information on making a better decision. But there are times that the questions become obsessive and intrusive as you begin to doubt how or even if you should move forward.

Many times, after a failure, you can start to question how and why you failed. Not just assessing it, but assigning blame for it. Too often, the blame is our own. That thought process, if given too much life, makes you doubt that you can succeed at something or even anything. Doubt can be a morphing compilation of an array of emotions that will keep you transfixed in one spot. Stuck! At some point, you have to stop asking the questions and make a decision. Not fearfully, not regretfully, nor insecurely. Make the decision and then own it. There is the responsibility that accompanies all the decisions you make. If you don't fear failure, you can accept responsibility then remove doubt to sustainable success.

I have watched individuals who were filled with doubt—unable to correct their behavior—begin to lose all perspective of their surroundings. Each day they were spinning with thoughts of indecision and fear. This is not the way to take advantage of an opportunity or position yourself for success. You have to drive yourself to make each minute count and not waste time second-guessing everything. Think, research, get good counsel, but mitigate your doubt and make decisions to get things done today. Now is your time for forward-thinking and leaving doubt behind. Remember, time is ticking.

.

CHAPTER 4

BE AUDACIOUS

"Difficult and painful as it is, we must walk on in the days ahead with an audacious faith in the future."

Martin Luther King, Jr.
Civil Rights Leader

Au·da·cious (ô-dshs) adj. *1. Fearlessly, often recklessly daring; bold. 2. Unrestrained by convention or propriety; insolent.*

Many believe that to be dynamically successful, you can do so without any significant change. I have never seen anyone who has attained great success and, in some measure, not change. Let me say that changing does not have to be negative, but change will happen. Yes, you may keep the core of who you are, but success brings its own set of changes. Being the same person that you were when you began the journey toward success and at the end of your trek does not usually happen. All the experiences in between change you. The many trials and obstacles you've overcome to get to the top of the mountain are not soon forgotten. They often make and define you.

When I speak about being audacious, it is not the rude, cocky, or boastful type of brashness that offends people. This can and will be a distraction to your success and the development of sustainable partnerships. The definition of audacious that I'm referring to is deliberate boldness that comes from an inner strength to keep going in the face of adversity. It is a demonstrated measure of resilience. To stand when others sit. To speak boldly while others are silent in the face of conflict. It takes ignoring opposing views or avoiding negative distractions while being willing to stand alone while others walk by or walk away. It's more than your understanding that you may have to be in early or stay late (or oftentimes both) to carry your dream to fruition.

People follow the audacious. Why? They follow because those individuals have boldness, past expectations, and little problem striving for excellence and are often going someplace. Nobody wants to follow someone who is just walking in circles or on some aimless path toward an endless dream. People like to follow those that have a destination and a plan.

I think of Apple Computer Founder Steve Jobs and media mogul Oprah Winfrey as truly audacious people. They never fit in anyone's box, but always were pushing past all expectations to achieve over and over again. Every time they have been in the public eye, they were embarking on a new, challenging, and exciting venture. You came to expect that they would push through and expand boundaries to make life more exciting and livable.

If being average is your goal, then strive for that. But if you dare to live in the full capacity of who you are, then you are going to have to do more. The thought that you can see a goal, believe in it with all your might and passion, make it your ultimate focus, defy what others say and think, while diligently moving toward it; well, that is audacious.

Wake up each day with the intentional boldness and tenacity to fight all those that say your dream is too big or too hard, including that critic in your own mind. Others may think you are too young or too old, not educated enough, the wrong type, or it's simply not your turn. Defy them. Many may scoff at your ability to dream and have passion for more extraordinary personal accomplishment. There are always going to be individuals that have a low expectation of themselves, and consequently they won't believe anything significant could happen for you. They will always say that "you can't," "you shouldn't," "be careful," or "watch your step."

You may find that your success will make others feel uneasy and even threatened is as if their words are snares plotting your demise. In your mind and when appropriate, from your mouth, you have to tell them to SHUT UP! Keep moving, and don't spend your time seeking their support nor approval. They are Drainers, as I've mentioned before. The power of knowing that you are going to make it is a bold way to think of each day. If you are going to be bold, truly audacious, then you must accept the fact that some people will like you and others won't. You don't have the power to dictate who likes or dislikes you.

For example, if you have typically been meek and unassuming, and suddenly now you are taking control of your life and beginning to act forthrightly in your words and actions, many will look at you quite differently. Being audacious is accepting that you will not always be liked or may sometimes be ostracized. Get accustomed to it and begin to change the people that you associate with, if needed.

So, where you stand in relation to others matters. I have heard it said, and it seems to be the case, that you are the average of the ten closest people that you associate with. You are slotted somewhere in the middle. If your people tend to be outgoing, progressive, and purposeful, then you stand a greater chance of being more like them. If they are fearful, lack confidence, and want to remain underachievers, you will have a place over there with them. Stand firm and associate yourself with those who are going where you want to go or, better yet, have already arrived.

You want to place yourself in a position where you are getting stretched. If you are always the smartest one in the room, then you are in the wrong group. In separating yourself from others, a level of contention may build, but you must readjust, nonetheless. Some may talk, obstruct and yes, even lie to and about you. But if you are serious about developing yourself and sustaining your success, then you must learn to toughen up.

Building success daily—your personal 1440—should bring you out of the shadows, into the light. The ability to see yourself shifting is essential and part of the process. You have fully seen success for yourself to be able to plot your way forward. No professional athlete ever won a championship without dreaming about it and seeing victory. It irritates me when an athlete says, "We will do our best, and may the better team win." Be audacious and say what you planned for and mean. Say, "We are the better team and plan to win decisively and take the championship." I don't start something, hoping to come in second. I may come in second, but first was always the plan.

It is quite often said, "success breeds contempt." Those words are right. Success can bring the best, but quite often, it brings the worst out of people. You will find that your success will make others feel uneasy and even threatened, but there is nothing you can do about it. You can't un-succeed to make them happy or feel better. Your success is not tied to how others think about you. Part of being successful, in some respects, can be somewhat selfish and self-serving. It doesn't necessarily mean being evil or nefarious, but rather focused and deliberate. If your success is contingent on someone else's joy, then as their joy goes, so does your success.

We all want to receive some level of personal reward from our hard work and feel good about it. Feeling good about our accomplishments is not a bad thing. A victory lap is O.K. It is not arrogance but a heightened level of confidence that lets you and others know that you are at the top of your game. For example, it is like knowing that you are better prepared than another competitor bidding on a project, and have a great expectation of winning. Losing is not an option when success is the expectation.

The time that it takes to prepare and focus on a deliberate plan is a valuable commodity that you can't waste. Audacious means that you can tell others that you are good at what you do, and you back up that fact consistently. Do this by making sure that you deliver on what you promised and live up to expectations.

In order to keep audacity from becoming arrogance, it is important to remember to balance your success with a measure of humility, a soft tone, and genuine care for others—even for your adversaries. Success may create enemies but don't make enemies for success's sake by being arrogant. Be humble, empathetic, and willing to understand other perspectives; audacious is not arrogant.

CHAPTER 5

SIGHT ADJUSTMENT

*"You are never really playing an opponent.
You are playing yourself, your own highest
standards, and when you reach your limits,
that is real joy."*

Arthur Ashe
Tennis Star, Humanitarian

You dreamed big when you were little. Without a care in the world, nor any apprehension as to what life would bring, you might have believed you could be anything. You may have aspired to be an astronaut, doctor, lion tamer, or racecar driver. There probably was nothing outside the realm of your reality or possibility. You reality might have been so grand that some of you might have even thought that one day you would even fly.

But, as you matured, reality had a way of transforming your dreams into something quite different. In fact, life's twists and turns have the potential to alter your view of reality, either positively or negatively. With a more mature reality in hand, you probably re-assessed your goals or made new ones.

In addition, the path to seeing your goals and dreams accomplished changed over time as well. When you were young, it seemed like all you had to do was visualize your path and it would all come true. It seemed so simple. Come up with a plan and start moving toward the result with little concern as to the obstacles that were not a part of your plan. You had your sights aligned on what you wanted, and thought you knew the best way to attain it. But the obstacles came.

It is sight alignment that drives you consistently toward your dreams, but you may find that you lack the resolve to overcome obstacles consistently. There are supposed to be bumps in the road, holes that you fall into and have to dig your way out. Opposition is always the plan for the day. Make no mistake about it. Things that stand in your way should always make you more determined to acquire success and to not give up. Most times you can't avoid the obstacles, but you do have to navigate them well.

I was once told that if you can't see it, you can't hit it. That sounds simple enough. It was the advice a football coach once gave me as I was learning to be a better tackler. He noticed at practice one day that as I got closer to the offensive player coming my way, preparing for a hit, I closed my eyes. Sometimes I would make the hit and other times it would be a clear miss.

The coach ran the play over and over and was amazed at my blind attempts. He said, "What in the world are you doing?" (I think there were some other choice words from him as well.) "If you don't see the other player, how are you going to hit him?" I said that I got as close I could and hoped for the best. His disdain was obvious. He took me off the field and continued with the practice. As I sat on the sideline, I knew clearly why I closed my eyes. I was afraid! Afraid of what was coming my way. I wanted to do well, but not at the expense of seeing what was coming.

The next day at practice the coach said, "Here comes Ray Charles." I somehow knew he was talking about me. I got on the field, and wouldn't you know it, the play was coming my way. Again, hoping for the best, eyes closed as the running back turned the corner, with inches to go he spun, dipped, and well you know the rest. Just at that point as I raised my head, in the midst of defeat, I saw the cheerleaders moving to our side of the field for their practice. They paused to observe. The coach said, "Ray, here we come again." Determined not to be embarrassed in front of the cheerleaders and beginning to get more than irritated and focused on making any mark, I was determined to see it through to the end.

Everything now was moving in slow motion. I could hear the quarterback's cadence as the running back got the ball and took the corner at top speed. This time—intentionally and with my eyes wide open—I saw something that I had never seen before. His eyes were closed. He was afraid of being hit, and right before he got hit, he closed his eyes. At that split moment, I let out a warrior yell and hit him right between the numbers. It was the best tackle of my life, and to put the icing on the cake, he fumbled the ball. But to my dismay, I was so focused on the battle I did not notice that my motivation, the cheerleaders, all had their backs turned away from the field the entire time. Go figure!

I learned a valuable lesson from that experience. Your sight can and most likely will be hindered in some way by the fear of contact with the opposition on route toward your destiny. You will inevitably have to cross some sort of conflict that is yours to tackle. No one else will be there to fight these battles for you. You have to look the future right in the face, stare it down, and take control of the situation.

You just can't close your eyes and hope for the best. That becomes chance or even worse, dumb luck.

Don't rely on luck or chance, as they are not part of your plan for success nor are they a reliable solution in times when you need definitive outcomes. You have got to adjust your sight each day on what it is that you are trying to accomplish. Just as I thought that I was overmatched facing this opponent, the truth of the matter was my opponent was the overmatched one. By adjusting my sight and removing my fear I could see that.

You may get into a race for superiority because of your own sense of inferiority. You may do things and try to prove yourself to people who really don't matter. What is it that you are trying to accomplish? And when you get it, why are you so disappointed?

For example, great archers know that distance, terrain, and wind are elements that can be obstacles that may hinder the effectiveness of hitting a target. Defining and realigning your sight is key in hitting the archer's and your target, which for you is your life's goal. If your sight is off even by a fraction, you can find as time goes on the distance between you and your goal can be vast. You may think you see it, but you can't attain it. What then do you do? You refocus your sight. What was the original target? Do you see it? Adjust for factors that affect hitting your target: time and distance. What is the timeframe you are working with, and how far away are you from the target?

Let's say, for example, that the target is to be a senior partner of your firm within five years. Now seven years have passed, and you have not made it. You have made strides and a lot of motion, but it seems to be of little consequence. You have little choice but to reassess your situation and decide what the next step will be.

First, you have to assess if this is something that you still want. You may look at something early on in life, and it might seem that if you could just get it, all would be good. Life is a funny thing. Twists and turns come, and what was once the pinnacle of attainment is merely another steppingstone. Time and situations do change, and they are unavoidable.

If you didn't get the position, you have three choices. You can wallow in grief and despair at not being where you want at this time in your life. It can involve blaming others for your missed opportunity and station in life. That won't help and will create other issues.

You could kick it in gear and do all the things that you didn't do on the path up the ladder, realizing that it will take time and an ultimate commitment to relight things, gather yourself, and move forward. If that is the case, then do it. If those two aren't the direction you want to go, then there is another option.

You can look at it as a well-fought effort and refocus on other areas. Take inventory of how much was sacrificed to get to this point without attaining your goal. Was it a marriage, time with a child, a hope, or a dream? Make each day matter and get the best out of your experience. No matter the path you choose, you can't be burdened by past missed accomplishments. That is a waste of time. All you can do is create new expectations and set your sights on them.

Once you have experienced a major setback, you can plan more realistically for a new goal. You can start a new trek, a journey worth taking and conquering, using a new sight adjustment to maintain your focus and keep on track. But, this time you will be more attuned to look for the obstacles and plan for the distractions while you appreciate the journey. It may even be the journey that brings the greatest satisfaction and reward. It will demonstrate the strength and resilience you have at seeing the light at the end of the tunnel and fighting your way to getting there. After all, you are battling for your success!

Weapons of War – Your Tools For Success

For any battle, preparation is the order of the day. You first must know your opponent and the tactics needed for your defense and their defeat. No battle is worth fighting if there are no spoils. Before you get into the battle be sure that the fight is worth the effort, pain, and the possibility of loss. No, I am not advocating your defeat, but to get into a battle you must be willing to give it your all. Giving your all is the minimum of what you have to lose or gain. But even in a loss, there is a lot to be learned by the experience. As you begin to read about this battle process, let's determine if this is an offensive or defensive confrontation. There is a difference.

Offensive Battle

An offensive battle is often thought of as an attack first, with force and dominance for a swift victory.

The weapons of warfare for an offensive battle are much different than defensive ones. The ability to know when and where an attack will take place is a most cherished commodity. Whether attacking a business deal, leveraged buyout, or making a career move, you will need weapons adaptable enough to sustain you. As an offensive battle, you get to choose the time and place to attack. Your weapon could be education, allies, insight, and experience. You will have the opportunity to determine how and when to use them. The best weapon in your arsenal will be the research you have obtained from watching that thing you are going to attack. You can assess weak points and gain an opportunistic advantage. You must be decisive, deliberate, and engaged if you are going to be on the offensive.

The Offensive Plan - Weapon 1

A well-thought-out plan is the foundation of your offensive weaponry. As you begin setting your goals and objectives, you should have a reasonable idea of the direction you're going. The main objective is getting to your destination as smoothly and as quickly as possible. You can't overlook the obstacles that may present themselves. Map out the path and list all obvious and obscure obstacles that could be in your way. Ensure that you understand the time that it will take to implement your plan. Timing can be everything in making or breaking your plan.

Remember the 1440? If you are moving too fast you may lose attention to detail and waste time having to regroup and miss opportunities. Move too slowly and you may bring all great intentions to a screeching halt. Keep in mind that you will constantly adjust your resources or use them as you assess your plan.

For example, I have always been and forever will be a diehard fan of the Dallas Cowboys. The ultimate experience for me has been to see them play a live game. Now, that has been quite a struggle to pull off, no matter how much battle planning has been completed, including ticket purchase, food prep, and getting everyone ready for game day. I know the most direct and quickest way to heaven, or as it is more widely known, Cowboy Stadium. However, all that planning really doesn't matter. Someone riding in the car always delays us. And, once I leave the confines of my semi-controlled home environment and drive into the crazy, unpredictable Dallas traffic, I know I have to pull out my tactical resources and check the GPS for alternate routes. In this battle, I refuse to let the traffic deter me. I move on. Time is ticking. And heaven is waiting.

Assembling a Team – Offensive Weapon 2

One of the most important lessons I was ever taught was that you can't do it all by yourself. Success alone is success unfulfilled. If you are to do anything of great consequence and lasting value, it will take others to play a role in your success. There is no true team that works when individuals are not locked into a team process. Individuals never win it all, teams do. You have to be secure enough in your ability that you can assemble individuals around you that may be more talented, more experienced, or just better than you.

The value of a team is when each team member shares a common goal while utilizing unique strengths and abilities of others in the group to acquire the goal. Teams need multidimensional motivation to keep everyone willing to push to the end. Are you the type of leader/teammate that comes in late and won't pull your weight? Or will you come in early prepared and leave late when the work is done? Can you do it while inspiring others toward greatness? Are you a person who will hold up a struggling team member or let them fall and fail?

The team mentality is contagious and often the difference between some occasional wins and sustainable success. All of this doesn't occur by happenstance, but by using every minute of every day to get the best out of each other and yourself.

Defensive Battle

There are some simple things that you need to know about an attack coming your way. Was the attack provoked, a reaction, or methodically planned? Were you prepared for the attack? How do you recover from it? You have to make sure that you develop a defensive posture for preparation, not paranoia.

The presence of sheer strength can many times be the only deterrent you need. But not always. In any defensive battle, you must be able to take a hit. You will get hit. Don't take it personally, even if the attack was meant to be personal. Defense is taking the hit, withstanding the onslaught of the offensive attack, and standing your ground. Yes, you will have to dodge and block some attacks, but at some point, you are going to get hit. That hit could be an attack on your integrity, a betrayal from an associate at work, or people just being people and attacking to acquire what you have. No matter the reason, get ready.

To prepare for success, you need to look at potential areas of attack. Spend your time working on skills and assessing the damage. Does the attack require a response, and if so, how would you respond to it? What areas would you attack? How vicious of an attack would you hit yourself with? That is how you develop your defense. If you have integrity issues, deal with the truth related to them and learn how to defend yourself. You need to develop a defensive strategy where you look at yourself as the opponent. How would you attack yourself? Knowing your vulnerabilities will give you a greater insight into what your defense should be.

Situational Awareness – Defensive Weapon 1
You go through each day with life happening around you. Most of the time you might be oblivious to what's going on that is not in your focal point. I have been at sporting events and have seen a dynamic play occur, then someone turns and says, "What happened?" I looked in total disbelief and wondered, "How could you have missed that? What are you here for?" They were either talking, texting, tweeting, or doing something trivial and missed it.

How many times have you been in a meeting and looked away at your phone to answer an email, then looked up to see that you just missed it? Whatever your "it" is. Missing an opportunity because you weren't listening. Being distracted can make you miss great opportunities.

Situational Awareness is recognizing any threat or resource that may present itself in the early stages. You can take measures to avoid the danger and utilize the resources, but you have got to pay attention to your surroundings. If you are advancing in success, then situations will change.

One of the things that I enjoy is riding motorcycles. Though some may see the danger, I find comfort and freedom. Whenever I ride, I know that to stay alive I need situational awareness. What is around me that can harm me? What situations do I need to avoid? How do I not ride beyond my skill and ability so that I don't injure myself? What are my safety measures, and what is my avenue of escape? What have I prepared for? Have I maintained the tools of my success? All of these have gotten me out of some dire situations on the highway and in life.

Living each day in situational awareness allows for a different view of every situation you encounter. It won't let you fall into the trap of being apathetic or complacent. It is a state of mind and a way of living. As you enjoy each moment, you are keenly and constantly aware of what is going on and quite able, willing, and more importantly, prepared to respond effectively.

Planned Response – Defensive Weapon 2

People often talk about how they would act if a certain thing would happen. You have heard them before. "If that were to happen to me, I would…" For many, it is just talking, but for some, the talk is well thought out and methodical. It is a plan of action based on what has occurred. It is not just thought but direct action.

There is a quote by Publius Flavius Vegetius Renatus, commonly referred to simply as Vegetius, who was a military expert and writer for the Roman Empire. He said something I heard my mother say years ago, and I live by it today. He wrote, "In time of peace, plan for war."[6] That is a planned response. It is pre-existing, well planned, waiting to be executed.

I recently observed some workers installing a fire suppression system in a new office building. The sprinklers, smoke detectors, and fire alarm were all being installed in such a way as to not be intrusive or to impede the operations of the business, hidden in many respects. As I walked past a few days later the job was completed, and there was a tag on one of the fire alarms that said, "tested and approved." In essence, it was a planned response for any fire that may come. No matter the time, season, or opportunity, it was ready and, without any thought, would respond accordingly to mitigate any damage.

This is somewhat the way I enter a business meeting. I look at every conceivable obstacle or threat, and well beforehand I plot a response. There are options that I may never use. Like arrows in a quiver, ready for use when needed. I have planned responses for questions that were never asked, suppression for attacks that never materialized.

Planning this way was not wasted time, but preparation for success. Time is a commodity that can't be wasted, therefore when an opportunity comes your way you have to make the most of it and be ready for anything from sharks, vipers, leprechauns, and Martians (I mean anything, right?) to all the monsters of the world—all at the same time. Your planned response, like the fire suppression system, sits dormant until needed, but when needed, it responds with full force and precisely as planned.

This is where your strength of character is established. It lives in the background of your life, quiet and reserved. Your preparation and knowing that whatever situation you find yourself in you have the security to make the best of it. If things go wrong, as they sometimes will, you are ready for that. Make the best of it; learn.

Assessment of Resources – Offense and Defense Tactic

Never rest on your laurels. Always reload and diversify your resources. Rely on those things that give you an opportunity and an edge to move forward and protect yourself. Time is one of those things. The acquisition of relationships and overall knowledge allows you to use the time to regroup, rest and plan your next move. Sometimes this means taking some time to think of things from a different angle or perspective. Sometimes this means taking a break and experiencing something new, like new music or art. (In the Reference section at the end of this book, I've included a wide range of musical albums and artistic venues for inspiration).

Make no mistake; you can't stay in the same spot for very long. Time is an opportunity to see your way forward but may not always be your friend. It's not where you rest in a hammock, like you do on a vacation, but it's more like a NASCAR pit stop. Get what you need, adjust yourself, listen to good advice then get back in the race. Remember, your 1440 as you are in it to win it.

CHAPTER 6

RELENTLESS

"The drive to close the gap between near-perfect and perfect is the difference between great and unstoppable."

Tim S. Grover
Author

It is amazing how so many people start something dynamic in concept and scope, yet never finish. They begin with much fanfare and great exuberance, but when they move just a few steps in the right direction, they fizzle out and fail or roam aimlessly in the wrong direction. I often wonder how something so good can go so bad, so fast. It is not always the lack of planning or even intent, but the lack of attention to the minor details that could derail the accomplishment of a dream.

This was the case in the 2008 Beijing Olympics for the United States 4x100 men's relay team. This was the team to beat. The best of the best in the world. As this highly touted U.S. team sped to an early lead at the start and during the first and second baton pass, it was with great anticipation as the thousands in attendance and millions watching worldwide, prepared for a U.S. win. This was the one event that everyone was watching. Even people who didn't love track watched too. All that was left was the final pass of the baton, the final sprint, a dominating finish, crowd roar, and a gold medal celebration. It was not to be the case.

On the final pass between the third and fourth runners, the baton was dropped. An audible groan of anguish pierced through the live crowd and from television audiences around the world. The dream was not to be realized and all was lost. The race was a mere 38.31 seconds long.[7] A world record was set. But not for the favorite. All the practice and planning were gone in an instant. The gold medal and American/World sports immortality were shattered.

Thought to be one of the finest and fastest, the team came in with great expectations and promise. Each member of the team was quite accomplished in their own right and hand-picked to be on this all-world team. In preparation for this event, hundreds of hours of practice were spent on proper running form and execution at the start. An acute focus on health and total body fitness was a premium. Speed on the turn and the kick of the anchor runner was left to their pure gifted ability.

And then there was the baton: just shy of 12 inches in length and a mere 15 ounces, it was the only thing standing in the way of immortality. All that needed to be done was to hand off the baton to the next runner. Something that should have been easily done became the demise of an individual, a team, and a nation. It was the FAILURE to achieve the only goal the team set forth. You may see it as just some freak of nature or a one-time anomaly, but hours later the same day, the star-studded women's team, did the same thing. They too lost; failure.

This is too often the plight you will face at some point in your professional or personal journey. You may start well with great intentions, and somewhere along the way you might drop the baton and get sidetracked from your finish.

As I look at the makeup of a relay team, there are four roles on the team: The Starter, The Maintainer, The Planner, and The Finisher. Each plays a significant part in the completion of a task. In reality, to achieve the plans each of you have, you must be each of these at the appropriate time. You can't do it alone. You need to know when, where, and how to play the proper role and keep it all together.

The Starter - *Role I*

When you are a ***Starter,*** you have the mentality of getting out first. A starter is a self-directed and focused person who is instinctual and instantly ready. You merely await a sound; a moment to unleash all that is inside of you. The competition beside you doesn't matter. If you do your job, they don't exist. They just need to end up behind you. The race is the moment of anticipation that you have trained and sacrificed for. Distractions and false starts are not an option for you. You look left, then right, all the while focusing on getting out first and making your mark.

You must be faster than the competition and make a smooth transition to the next phase of success. This is the pattern that allows for a myopic view of things: self-centered, self-directed, and determined. But given all your effort, you cannot win at this phase of the race. You are not looking to finish, but to start well, strong.

You can lose the race by false starts, missteps, blunders, and lack of precision, but can't win it this way. Winning suggests that you must perform at a higher level and pass on what you have done this far. The question is, can you deliver what you have started until you reach your next role? Pass the baton.

The Maintainer - *Role II*

The ***Maintainer*** has the heart of determination. This is the role you play on your journey where you truly find out not only who you are but what you are made of. Many start a good journey, but too few finish. Is it any wonder that there are many more freshmen entering college each year than seniors graduating? Many things happen along the way that can interrupt the ultimate goal of a college degree; on time.

So, then what does it take to maintain? TRUE GRIT! There is a poem by Rudyard Kipling called "If" and the second stanza begins with some important, life-challenging, provocative thoughts that must be observed by those who wish to maintain.

> *If you can dream - and not make dreams your master;*
> *If you can think - and not make thoughts your aim;*
> *If you can meet with triumph and disaster*
> *And treat those two imposters just the same;*
> *If you can bear to hear the truth you've spoken*
> *Twisted by knaves to make a trap for fools,*
> *Or watch the things you gave your life to broken,*
> *And stoop and build 'em up with worn-out tools....*[8]

It is in these mere verses that success rises or falls. It shows the ability not to be dissuaded by contrary voices and obstacles that are true or imagined. It is having failure look you straight in the face and tell you that victories are failures and failures are a disgrace. And yet, you press on. You have to realize that far too many give up too early in the race. You feel the pain of disappointment and fatigue of not having quick success.

Nothing created to be longstanding will mature overnight, nor will it be eternally appreciated without resilience. The level of success that you want to attain will push you toward your capacity.

You may not want to go and through the pain, you don't want to feel it. There you will find the endurance to stay strong through tough times. It's more than getting up early in the morning and staying late at night. You have to learn on the fly and keep moving. It will be like changing the oil in a car while it's going down the highway at 80 mph. A pain here and cramp there means absolutely nothing for someone who is going somewhere. Limp if you have to, wobble, twist, whatever it takes to make it. There is no rulebook hidden somewhere that says success is pretty. Sometimes it comes in awkward stages, but you must maintain and take control. Pass the baton.

The Planner — *Stage III*

The **Planner** is involves being methodical in thought and action. This is where you have the option to look back and see what has been or what is happening now. You can assess whether you are ahead or behind and make slight positional adjustments. This is the position that sets up for the win, but will never cross the finish line. The mindset of a planner, in this setting, is one that will take a calculated risk as to how to proceed. The competition is visible and coming at great speed. The planner must decide in a fraction of a time how to proceed.

You know that someone or something is coming after you to finish. You have to position yourself to give the finisher the best opportunity to win. That is the role of the planner. It is almost like watching a basketball game where there is an awesome alley-oop dunk. One player is throwing the ball to a place where the other will be. Time and opportunity meet, and there is a score, but the one throwing the ball doesn't get the points, just an assist. It is a true partnership in motion. Pass the baton.

The Finisher - *Stage IV*

The **Finisher** is just that; when you are in this role you have the unique ability to finish strong and first at any cost. When you are here, you cannot doubt your ability, nor your role in the race. You Finish! It is supreme confidence, bordering on arrogance, tempered by humility knowing that you are just one part of the whole. It is here, that you know that if you can get the baton in one more hand, nothing can stop you from winning.

Here, you will not attempt to pace yourself. You have only one gear–all out. This is a gear that success determines you must possess and use effectively. When the opposition is around you and you have done everything else and still are not finishing, you have to push further and faster. You have to develop a finisher's kick.

I have had the opportunity over the past few years to work closely with a wide array of highly astute college students. I have seen them work with great intensity in the first two years to get established and make their mark. The junior year is an opportunity to set everything in motion to position themselves toward graduation. But somehow, for many of them, the transition toward senior year gets to be one of drudgery, life's conflicts, and mis-directions. They are so close but lack that last kick to finish.

Life is the same way. Your drive was there in the beginning, but now life happened. Financial, family, career, and relational issues have crept in, and the desire and energy to finish are waning. This is the mentality that MUST be halted and redirected. As you look back at the accomplishments of any of life's races you've begun, it is apparent that you have invested too much time just to give up now. The finish line is closer than you think. If you can dig deep and begin to kick, you can finish.

This is your only option. Dig deep to finish that college degree or start that new business. Giving up is the easy part, but far too often comes with a lifetime of regret. Finishing is an accomplishment that can't be taken away. Each finish is the stepping-stone to the next plateau of your journey. Set your mind on finishing strong every day and making sure that during your 1440 you always have that extra gear and always ready to kick to the finish.

Now as you look at all 4 stages, you see how the Starter, Maintainer, Planner, and Finisher work as independent roles, as well as complete a team. You must look at each day and plot a path to the finish, all the while looking at the start, maintenance, planning and how are you going to finish strong and win. As days move to weeks and months to years, your internal team will begin to have many more finishes and wins. Take the time to pat yourself on the back for each of these, and don't take them for granted. Wins are not always easy to come by. For the success you want, you must make it through all four stages within the time you have. **<u>Finish STRONG!</u>**

CHAPTER 7

THE AFTERMATH

"If you're not practicing, somebody else is, somewhere, and he'll be ready to take your job."

Brooks Robinson
Baseball Hall of Famer

There are certain events or challenges that may define a point in history or a significant time in your life. This situation changes life as you have come to know it. In December 2004, the world looked on with utter shock at the sights and sounds of a devastating tsunami in Phuket, Thailand and responded with their hearts and wallets. People's genuine compassion for the loss of life and property moved them to action. The carnage was so shocking that words could not embrace it.

But as time passed and other news stories took over, the moment that was beyond words has soon faded into a distant memory. The focus was gone, and it was relegated to just another historical event of days gone by. Those that have a firsthand experience of enduring events, they often have no escape from it. The storm is over but there is an Aftermath. *Aftermath – (Noun) 1: the consequences of an event (especially a catastrophic event).*[9]

The aftermath defies all time and logic. Often there is no outer sign of the remnants of the inward struggle. You may go through a divorce, the death of a loved one, bankruptcy, illness, or incarceration. They are all issues that people go through every day and find themselves on the other side. The storm is over, the sun is shining, and the birds are singing, but you are oblivious to all of this. Almost stunted in position.

People have short memories of the pain of others particularly when things don't personally affect them. They often ask the question, "Aren't you over that yet?" "Over what?" They will whisper while you are away, "What's wrong with them? That situation was so long ago." It's not a "what or a when" but a morphing configuration of what we reflect on as "was." It is hard, in fact impossible, to live in the past and the present at the same time. Your mind is a great processor of both good and bad information. You process it equally, but not always efficiently or effectively. It is in the process that the lines get blurred, and you can walk into a zone of unbelievable despair and confusion. How do you get out? How did you get in? Where do you go from here? How do you deal with the aftermath?

Don't think that bad things only happen to you. It is easy to think that you are the only one in your situation and begin to throw yourself a pity party and dread the world. This is not the case. Every minute spent dwelling in the past is a moment you don't live for your future, or even see it. People go through crazy situations every day. You just don't know it. Every so often there is a story on the news about a perfectly balanced individual that has a meltdown, totally loses it, and does something so outlandish that it defies understanding. Everyone around them always says that "they seemed normal."

The reality is that many of you have experienced things in life that you have not let go of yet. Events and circumstances may keep you burdened as you contain our emotions just to get by. The hope is that no one notices. You think if they find out, it will affect how you are thought of or treated.

You need to transition from this temporary place. If you don't, it will seem as if there is no way in or no way out. The original event was some time ago, but you somehow are still living in fear, anguish, and stuck in the aftermath. It is a place that no one wants to go to, and few find their way out of. So why do you seem to find yourself in that place? It is not a planned trip nor were you prepared to go there. There is a way to deal with the aftermath of all of your situations; deal with the truth of it.

If you planned poorly on several business ventures, extended your credit, pushed past all financial wisdom, and failed through bankruptcy. Well, you failed and went bankrupt! That is the truth; admit it. Put on your big boy or girl pants and keep moving. You are not the first and won't be the last to fail.

It goes the same for divorce, natural disasters, family issues, and life's heartbreaks. You have to wake up the next day and move on. The aftermath is not a place to take up residency. You will have pain, frustration, and endless questions, but don't stop moving forward. Every time you stop you allow memories to take over and control the situation. You can have memories while you move forward. If you stop for too long, memories become a distraction from what is supposed to take place today.

Use the circumstances of life to create an aftermath that is positive and life-sustaining. Take each day as an opportunity to have a small victory. For some, it will be just getting through it without crying, for others not cussing. For many, it will be to walk the path of forgiveness of others and self. Many have lost themselves, their true identity, throughout dealing with an array of issues in life. As you get a grip on the past and put it all in perspective, it allows for rational thinking for the future. Take control of your thinking and your future. The past is the just that, the past. All accomplishments or failures are in the past. You can't change it, nor remove it. All you can do is deal with it, learn from it and survive for a better day. Your issues in the past can be the stepping-stones toward success. They are the reminders of how strong you were to get through the situation, survive and move on.

Your success in dealing with any aftermath situation may not look like other successes. There will not be a ticker-tape parade nor accolades from your peers. These become personal, private victories and patting yourself on your own back to say, "Well done." Don't look for others to understand but recognize that you are minute by minute conquering the past while forging your dynamic future.

CHAPTER 8

WHO ARE YOU
LISTENING TO?

"People will feel safer around you and speak truthfully to you when they feel you are listening intently to them."

Brian Koslow
Author

The first house my wife and I purchased was in Gadsden, Alabama. A two-bedroom ranch on a hill built in the 1940s that needed a lot of work. I can recall on one occasion the plan for the day was to install a ceiling fan in our bedroom. It is something my wife long asked me to do. Simple enough. Go to the big-box hardware super-center, pick out the ideal fan, install it and the rest of the day would be mine.

As I began to take down the light fixture there was a voice asking, "Did you turn off the power?" My response was "Of course." I mean, "I know what I'm doing." The voice again, "Did you turn it off from the breaker?" My answer, "No, from the switch." Once again, "Of course, I know what I'm doing." Somewhere in the midst of connecting the wires, I left the room a few times, and maybe, as a creature of habit, I flipped the switch on the wall. Back up the ladder to finish the job, make sure the wires are screwed tight.

Did you know that touching live wires and metal could close a circuit? Well yes, it does! It was a quick shock that bounced me off the ladder to the floor. My wife, hearing a thud, wondered what was going on. "What was that?" My response, "Nothing, dear." The question to myself, "Why didn't I just listen?"

Most of the time you may not want to or just won't listen to anyone that has the sense to set you on the right path. Listening requires a lot of skill and discipline that most people have not taken the time to master. One of the greatest causes of failure is not listening to sound advice.

The art of listening, needed for success, should be from a diverse set of perspectives that offer something that positively and dramatically impacts the direction you are going. Don't just listen to all the cheerleaders in your corner. They will tell you just what you want to hear, the way you want to hear it. Perhaps your mother is not the best person to ask if she thinks you're cute. Every mother thinks that her child is cute, and as we all have seen, some are not.

Types You Listen to:
Cheerleaders –

As I just mentioned, cheerleaders tend to be family members or friends that love you unconditionally. They may not have a firm grip on the reality of who you are and what you need. They will tell you what you want to hear and wouldn't want to hurt your feelings.

These individuals can be unintentionally dangerous on an unparalleled level. They are by no means objective and try to protect you rather than propel you toward your destiny. The applause can be intoxicating. Don't forget that cheerleaders get paid to cheer no matter the condition or the score. Watching and listening to cheerleaders is no indication of whether you are failing or succeeding.

To prove my point, there was one night when I was at an NBA game as the home team began to get behind in the score. As usual, the cheerleaders cheered. And, as I continued to watch it was apparent they had a well-scripted routine that had no relationship to what was happening on the court. As the lead expanded to 22 points, the cheerleaders were on a pace of frenzied excitement, and their team on pace for a dramatic loss. They continued to smile and cheer. To listen to them was a contradiction of the truth. The fact was their team lost by 24 points. There was nothing to cheer for but cheer they did. Cheerleaders are at their best when they cheer. That is their only job. To make you feel good about the game, not the result.

Fans –

I am not ashamed to say that I am and will always be a Dallas Cowboys FANATIC! I have been one from long before they had a 15-1 record. Yes, that would be 15 losses and 1 win in the 1989 season. From that point to the multiple Super Bowl titles, I have been a fan without regard to any reality whatsoever. Every year they are good enough to win it all, and when they don't, next year will be better. When they won, they were the better team; and when they lost, they were still the better team, but the opponent just got lucky and beat us, usually by cheating. I have no rationale for believing my team's talent level could be less than others. The Cowboys are just great, and the quicker you recognize it the better. 'Nuff said!

Fanaticism is a state of mind that most often is not based in reality. You want to be applauded when you do well and often seek the affirmation of a job well done. You must be quite careful about how you listen to your fans. I have never seen a good parent look at their child and say that another's child is cuter or smarter. Sitting next to a baby genius, you will always contend that your child is still the smarter of the two. No fact, no reality, just a blind look at their own and negating the rest. This is a FAN.

The danger comes when you begin to build a foundation based on what the fans say. If they say that you are smart, better, or even great, then you have something to live up to.

One mature step you can take is to assess your reality against the words of the fan. Granted, there are times that reality and the fan's opinions are on the same page, but even then, you both are looking at the situation from two dramatically different vantage points.

For instance, when you look at an athlete, business professional, or highly skilled person, you see the polished and finished product. Seldom do you see what goes into becoming more than average, or better yet, elite. Hidden to many are the sacrifices of time leveraged to train the mind and body to excel and push past the point of reason. You don't see the quiet moments where even subtle failure produces regret and tears are the motivation and momentum that is needed to propel them toward greatness. In those moments of great success, they might feel a level of inadequacy and thoughts of what they could have done better. The fan never sees this and has little appreciation for it. The fan thinks that it is all too easy for them. The fan thinks they are just gifted, and they don't have to even try hard to be great.

Peers –

It probably seems that you spend a lot of your time with those that are the most like you. You are drawn to those who are closely aligned financially, socially, culturally, and so on with yourself. The comfort is that there is some equality in the relationships and a somewhat safe place to associate. You most likely find that your conversations and life experiences are similar with your peers.

Then, the challenge becomes a competition to see who gets the newest car or makes upgrades to their house first. Then it moves on to a contest over who is the fittest, even if you have to resort to plastic surgery to look better. The competition is won by mere subjective points. It is all about who has the best-looking lawn or accumulates the most things. All in all, there is nothing of substance pushing these relationships.

If there is a problem, each in the group, all from the same mindset will have one train of thought of how to deal with a given situation. They often look to each other as a sounding board to receive the approval for decisions. The reality is they are all collectively acting as dumb as a box of rocks. If all of our peer group's experiences are the same and the frame of reference the same, how then do you get an objective vantage point for an intelligent opinion?

The peer group plateau is good if you are ready to settle down and coast through life. If your goals are met and your best is behind you, then this is not a bad place to be. Granted, I am not putting down the whole peer group, but if what you seek is more, then you have to be challenged. The challenge always comes from someone or something outside the comfort zone of a peer group. This is always the case when you want to get to a higher level.

You can't rely on someone with a theory of the next level of business, industry, and life. You want someone who has been there and battled the storms, made mistakes, and successfully survived. This is the type of person that is outside your peer group and may seem to be light-years ahead of you. You may be somewhat intimidated by them as it seems they have it all together and possess what you want and, more importantly, know the path to get there.

The question is "Are you willing to leave the comfort of your peer group to get it?" How about humbling yourself and sitting at the feet of another to glean the wisdom they may drop in mere conversation? How far outside of the group are you willing to go striving for your destination? You will most certainly have to tune your attention to another kind of conversation and develop an articulation of speech on a more purposeful level.

This is a guiding force on the pathway of development that most are not willing to undertake. Being around people who can push you past your expectations, knowledge, and experience can be the catalyst to your success. When I think of people like this I think of the internationally acclaimed financial expert Suze Orman. She is a guru of personal finance and instructs on what it takes to become financially responsible and stable. The one thing that is evident in all that she does is that she pushes people out of their comfort zones by challenging them to change their behavior and associations.

One of her quotes is, "In all realms of life it takes courage to stretch your limits, express your power and fulfill your potential. It's no different in the financial realm." This is so true. You must get your finances in line with your life each day.

Enemies –

I know I said to ignore your enemies in a previous chapter, but I was talking about ignoring their trash talk. Enemies can have some good insights about you if you are brave enough to tune into some of what they say. I like listening to enemies the most. You can tell the level of your gifting and destiny by the level of the attack that comes your way. A good enemy will have you sized up at all times. They know your strengths, weaknesses, and know-how, and where to attack. Listen to them. Don't follow, just listen. They will tell you about yourself. I was taught as a child, "No dog ever chases a parked car." You must be doing something for them to be chasing you.

You can get distracted when someone attacks you, your ideas, or the plans you have. Your first inclination is probably to get mad and put up a defense that they cannot penetrate. You begin to develop a posture to prevent others from hurting you. Somehow, you can obsess about how you can stop them from stopping you. Granted there are ways to battle enemies that can result in total and complete victory. The question you have to ask yourself is, "Is this battle worth the spoils?" "Is this the hill you want to die on?"

Often the answer is NO. The battle with an enemy will inevitably occupy your time and deplete resources in a way that would take away from the task at hand. Be sure there is something to gain other than pride. Total focus can't be attained in two opposing directions. You will have to focus on one while ignoring the other.

The greatest battle of the enemy is to get you focused on everything else rather than staying on and completing your course. The battle you wage is fighting through the intimidation, distractions, and obstacles placed in your path. View each as part of the journey, not as detours. Viewed that way you will prepare a plan for each of and when confronted be the aggressor, not the victim.

Change your mindset on how you view those who would be considered your enemy. Don't take an attack personally, though it may be their intent to harm you, nor be so overwhelmed by it that it paralyzes your ability to act, react or respond. Don't settle for becoming a second-rate success when you have the ability of greatness within you. Enemies have the unique ability to sharpen your skills and make you acutely aware that nothing worthwhile is going to be easy.

You must possess an intestinal fortitude that positions you to block the attack, counter it and take advantage. This all has to be done without losing your stride, integrity, or focus. Remember, that they are enemies, and their job is to obstruct and defy you. Don't expect anything less. Succeed in spite of them EVERY DAY! Lick your wounds, bandage, and gather yourself. Then check your resources and prepare for the next battle. You will have another 1440 to deal with tomorrow's battle.

Mentors –

None of you can walk this success journey alone, each of you needs a Sherpa as a guide as you scale the next mountain. You have to maximize the time together with mentors; their words are like gold. Pick up every nugget and squeeze out as much as you can from them. Mentors have the most cherished commodity of success, a journey's wisdom. It's not just that they say something, but they have the wisdom and timing to know why what, and when to say something. And when not to.

Yes, it's good to know that your boss has just taken credit for the hard work you've accomplished to over the past six months. The wisdom worth knowing and listening to will give you insight into why it happened and what to do. More importantly, when to do it, so that you survive and move forward and not react and destroy your success. Remember, it is about purpose and perseverance. The true path of sustainable success is a long journey. This is not a sprint, but rather, a marathon.

A good mentor teaches you how to position yourself to respond and not react. But like anything of great value, a good mentor relationship can be rare and sometimes hard to acquire. What a good mentor wants is the best for you. This person wants to impart wisdom to you so that you may grow.

One question you have to ask yourself is what are you willing to do to be mentored? Most mentors don't want to carry dead weight. They don't want whiners or individuals who focus on useless drama. You must prepare yourself to be humble enough to listen to correction and then bold enough correct your actions. A mentor wants to show you what you are capable of and plot a path for your success. The path may take you places you don't want to go and at a pace that can be too fast or too slow for your patience. Humility is forged in a relationship like this. It is that level of humility that creates great leaders.

The mentor/mentee relationship is not always a bed of roses. There are going to be bumps and detours in the road, but it is all in your favor. Don't be discouraged but embrace the journey. The destination is well worth it. You have to recognize that if you could have done it alone, you would have. None of us get to the top of anything without guidance and sound advice. All of us at one time or another need to be pushed or prodded to move toward greatness.

You can always fail by yourself. If you are not willing to be subjected to mentoring, then recognize that you are not ready to take the next step in your personal and professional career. Even more significantly, you are wasting minutes each day trying it alone.

It is incredibly important that you focus on maximizing your time with individuals that you can learn the most from. This is a discipline that you must adopt if you were going to be the very best version of yourself. There are no shortcuts to this. Many will try to watch videos, read books, and listen from afar. But there is no substitute for spending time with individuals in conversation to gain wisdom, understanding and direction for your life. That is the best utilization of your time and the most significant opportunity for sustainable success.

CHAPTER 9

NEEDING AIR

"Life isn't measured by the breaths we take, but by the moments that take our breath away."

Unknown Author

Have you ever gotten the wind kicked out of you? Or have you seen someone struggle to breathe? Have you seen or felt the desperation in those moments? You don't appreciate air as much as you should until you are gasping for it. You can live most of your life with little understanding of the significance or the need for fresh air. Air is essential for life, so why take it so lightly? You never long for it until you are gasping for it, the last opportunity, the last deal, the last whatever you are in desperate need of.

Successful Failure

How could it be that life is descending into chaos all around you but you are supposed to be successful? You look the part. The name on the door and position on your business cards say success. They—all the "theys"—look to you for advice and direction. You are the go-to person, so how could it be that there are cracks in your armor?

Most of the time you are successfully moving forward one step at a time but often backward two. You are so focused on the success image that you turn a closed eye to the areas of your life that set you up for your next fall. The height of success is greatly exaggerated compared to the inner turmoil that brews when failure looms. The only way to truly see the cracks in our armor is through the stress test.

When industry wants to find the limits of an object's strength, they perform a stress test to see how far they can bend, pull or abuse it before it breaks. Life is the same way. It will push, pull, press and expand you past all comfort. The reality is that you can't truly know your capacity if you have never been pushed to your limit. Granted, when it happens you will want it to stop or slow down long enough for you to catch your breath. Take a quick breath, because life is not going to wait for you to get ready. Live Ready!

Secrets

Dictionaries have several definitions for the word "secret." As an adjective, it is said to be something "kept from the knowledge of any but the initiated or privileged." The noun speaks about it as "something that is or is kept secret, hidden or concealed." They are both right, but it doesn't stop there. It's not just that there is merely a secret, but it is in the way the secret is kept.

What are the secrets you keep so far hidden that you often lose track of them? Not the ones that if found would just be embarrassing, but those that would destroy who and what you are. Those inner, personal mess-ups and situations that you have stopped thinking about and convinced yourself that they may not even have happened. You may find yourself happy when you get through another day without someone finding out. What is it about this type of complex failure that makes you so insecure that you become disabled as you carry this burden of secrecy? You might have built a life of lies as a placeholder for your secrets. Lies that cover and conceal, but ultimately are building a foundation destined for utter and complete failure. A secret, hidden long enough, deep enough, becomes a burden beyond measure. The weight is truly crushing. This is your own personal curse.

Kept secrets are almost always only important to the one holding them, you. To most others, it is just a bump in the road, a little setback. To you, it has become a defining moment, sealed in time, etched in your memory, held with all your might. But why? Why do you keep it so close?

Why does it mean so much and hurt so badly? A childhood abuse; an adolescence letdown; an unforgivable word spoken by an unrepentant family member; personal, public, and private failures; unacceptable behavior; and abandonment are all placed in our treasure chest of secrets. These don't even begin to scratch the surface of the mire of things that you hide in the lockbox of deception and deceit. You all have something. Perhaps not to extremes, but something, nonetheless.

You have spent the better part of your life living with it. Now is the time to deal with it, control it and use it as the fuel that will propel you toward sustainable success, rather than stalling or running in place as you have been doing. The problem with holding a longstanding secret is that it tends to define who you are and can to shape the way you think.

Instead, try to use those secret failures as landmarks of how not to fail in a particular area. Don't let them be a destination that you strive toward. Correcting a failure may not erase a past incident, nor may correction give you the joy you were expecting. Getting past all of this, you will encounter emotions that are usually pushed aside or ignored. These becomes the last things that you want to deal with.

What you need at this point is to focus on forgiveness. This seems counterintuitive, but it's needed for you to move on. This forgiveness extends to what others have already done and what they might do to you in the future. It even cast a net over the forgiveness you need to give yourself for what you have done.

I have seen too many people get caught in the hurt and pain of what happened to them. They begin to look for someone, a villain, a business, a teacher, or a family member they can assign as a place to put and perpetuate their anger. This type of anger will exist and thrive until you release them and yourself from it.

As I have grown, I have found that unforgiveness is a complete waste of time. People will do you wrong. They will lie, cheat, steal and abuse you. Some encounters will be for reasons that may make sense, and others just for spite. Either way, you can't hold onto the bitterness and anger and expect to move past it. You can't allow what people do to you or situations that happen to you to hinder and stifle your growth. Strive to forgive, learn from the situation, and, ultimately, move on in a timely fashion. This is a hard thing to do but the very best option. You must move on and recover because there are going to be other situations that will come in the future.

I have learned that there is a resilience that one must have to continue. To continue believing in dreams, pushing ahead and finishing. I've often wanted to give up. Or found ways to convince myself the path that I was on wasn't really worth it or did not deserve my time. Both were wrong. But somehow I was convincing myself of it. It was at that point that one of my mentors challenged me. In fact, pushed me so hard that I wanted to resist all his advice in guidance. But he was right. His one word to me was **finish**! He told me the only way to finish at the end is to finish every day. That's what you must do. Every day finish. With obstacles, failures, insecurities, and times when you don't have the energy or mindset to continue. Finish! And finish strong! Make the time for it.

CHAPTER 10

STAGES OF LIFE

"There is one kind of robber whom the law does not strike at, and who steals what is most precious to men: time."

Napoleon
Emperor of France

The most intriguing part of life is the never-ending search for our next step. If you had all the answers to life's path, you would never hesitate and would move with grace and certainty. But it is not that simple.

I have divided life's journey into four stages that should ultimately lead you to your destination. What you want at the end of your journey is to be significant. You want to matter. You want to know that beyond all the stuff, the accolades, trophies, and relationships, that you did well and made a significant difference in the lives of others. But you have to grow to that point; you just don't start there. I wish I could. Ain't gonna happen! That being said, let's go to stage one.

Survival

Most of you have found yourself, at some point or another, in a situation where you are just trying to get from day to day. What was once in your control now seems out of control and under siege.

I remember in late 2007 as the financial system of the country not only went upside down but inside out. Hundreds of thousands of people didn't know what the next day would bring. Turning on the TV only showed foreclosures, bankruptcies, and joblessness. The biggest and most successful financial institutions were on the brink of disaster. Many thought the world was coming to an end. Everything that many thought of as being safe and secure was now in turmoil. Even people who were financially well off and with nothing to fear went into total panic mode.

I found that the panic mode transcended race, age, gender, socioeconomic standing, or religious affiliation. People went into survival mode. They said things like, "If I can just get through this, then...," or "We will just ride out the storm." Many even got to the point of, "I don't think we are going to make it."

Life is a litany of survival modes and storms. Make the decision each day to recognize the obstacles that are coming your way, and plan a method of escape. Giving up is not an option. Even when the situation looks dire, position your attitude toward coping, clear thinking, and correction. This will allow you to think more objectively about how you see your situation and, more importantly, how you respond to it. The only way to get out of the survival stage is to begin to think differently about it.

On May 1, 2003, when Aron Ralston left home for a day of climbing, I'm sure he had no idea to what extent he would have to use a different thought process to survive. Amputating your arm with a blunt knife is a task the average person would find virtually inconceivable. But on that unassuming day, it was the only option left to Aron after an 800-pound boulder fell on his arm, pinning it to a canyon wall. After five days, the little food and water he had were gone, and it was unlikely anyone would find him in the remote canyon in Utah.

In his book, "Between a Rock and a Hard Place", he describes how he managed to break free, first using the boulder to leverage his arm until the bones snapped and then sawing away at muscle and tendon with his pocketknife.[10] He then had to rappel down a 65-foot wall, get out of the canyon and seek help. He was walking back to his car when hikers found him.

It may seem that cutting your arm off is a bit drastic, but the situation called for survival or perish. He chose to survive. Every day you must decide to survive and move forward, no matter the situation of the day. Some day you will face a moment where a drastic decision must be made, but you will have to make it nonetheless. You will have to make up in your mind that survival means that you are going to do what it takes to become better and not bitter. I have seen people who have survived a very tough season of life, but have never risen above it. They get stuck in the memory of it and it consumes their life.

Recognize that the mere fact that you survived is an indication that there is more of life to come, and your journey has not ended. That being the case, you press toward the next stage of life: Stability.

Stability

Stability is the stage where things seem constant and consistent.

I can remember one summer as a teen when I took a ride on a friend's boat. This was my first experience on the open sea. They knew it was my first experience and warned me that if it gets too rough, I might get seasick. If I felt sick, I was to just say something, and they would slow down and find calmer waters. But as a brash teen, my ego took over, and I laughed at the notion of getting sick. Not me, I'm ready, let's go.

As we left the calm confines of the docking area, I knew all was well. This was a sunny day, and I had not a care in the world. With the sight of the shoreline fading into the backdrop suddenly the boat shifted, and the rear dropped. The two engines gave a thunderous roar, lifter the boat and we were off. We careened off wave after wave and moved into open seas.

All I could feel was the spray of saltwater and the hot sun from above, and then it happened. You know, that watery sensation in your mouth, the lightheaded dizziness that accompanies it. My ears were ringing, and all of the day's lunch had no desire to be contained. I couldn't speak, and all I could think was, "Lord, make it stop."

I slipped into a small, dark sleeping area in the front of the boat and thought that would help. We hit a string of big waves; the possibility of death crossed my mind. I just wanted it to stop. I guess they saw I was missing and came to find me. I could hear the laughter above as the boat slowed down. It seemed like an eternity, but soon we were back at the dock. I struggled to compose myself and get off that death trap. All I could wish for was stable ground.

The instability of life is quite like my boat ride. You may have this overconfident assertion that you can handle anything life can throw at you and when it begins to get rocky, you may get sick of it and want a place to go hide. What you need is a sense of stability in your life. You want your finances, friends, relationships, and business ventures to be stable enough so that you can relax. You may want a cruise control life. Now there is nothing wrong with wanting that, but sooner or later you are going to have to put on the brakes and use the steering wheel.

Changes are going to happen. Stability is nothing more than your ability to control the situations around you the best you can; holding all in your realm under submission. For instance, stable finances mean that you get your earnings in line with your expenses. It can mean learning to save and plan for retirement and making sure that you live within your means, making it a practice every day. It can also mean making wise decisions based upon detailed planning efforts.

Dave Ramsey, a financial guru, has a syndicated radio show with a tagline that speaks to this. He says, "It's about your life and your money."[11] This is so true. The balance of the two brings stability to each day. The stability rests in your ability to be disciplined in how you live your life. It is that thought process that allows you the opportunity to make the most of each day. You, like everyone, want to go through each day with minimal drama.

Success
Success is most often seen through the eyes of others. Many think that if you get the two cars, the corner lot house, the 2.5 children, and a dog, you have arrived. But arrive at what and where? The more stuff you get, the

more stuff you find you need to buy to support the stuff you already have. It seemed that at one point the car was the status symbol, then it was the right neighborhood, then the right club, then to be invited to the right events and parties. As if that was not enough, it now is all about who has the summer home, yacht, exotic destination vacations, and planes. Even after all of that, for many, it still is not enough.

I have had the great fortune to engage with many individuals who have all the stuff and more. They pass the success "eye test," meaning they look like they are successful from the outside. They appear to be the most successful and inspiring people you would want to meet. But, when I got closer to them and pulled back the curtain of their lives, I saw dysfunction and unhappiness. The "things" of success were a façade propped up to hide failures and to look good for others. They felt that looking the part was more important than actually achieving true success.

Success is not the stuff you acquire. Success is not how much money you can make, but how you live life with the money you have. Success is being able to make a marriage work or devoting time to being an active parent in your childrens' lives. Success feels like a peace of mind that comes from your accomplishments no matter how grand or small they are. Success is being content and enjoying the intangibility of achieving your goals.

Significance

This stage is not the end of life but, rather, a way of living after you have reached your goals. Significance is making sure that you do things that matter and make a substantive and positive difference in the lives of others. It is important that you remember that everything is not always about you.

Most of the previous stages are about you and how you get to be successful. But this stage is all about using all that you have acquired to make all you encounter better. You have spent a significant portion of your life working and now it is time to give back to those in the other stages on their success journeys.

I have watched individuals build an empire of wealth and influence and then end up losing it all or have it taken away. That is what I call a squandered lifetime. Unfortunately, it happens to more people than you may think. It happens because they stopped at success without achieving significance. They may have given some money to charities throughout their lifetimes, but maybe only to feel good about being named in an annual report or to get a position on the board. This is not significance. Significance is a planned development of life that allows you to passionately use your life as a tool that makes a difference for others.

Teddy Bruschi is one person who exemplifies significance.[12] Many may know of him as an All-American linebacker from the University of Arizona that was selected in the third round by the New England Patriots.

Bruschi went on to get two All-Pro selections, one Pro-Bowl selection, and three Superbowl championships with the Patriots. It sounds like a great success.

In February 2005, he suffered a stroke and returned to play later that same year earning him the NFL's Comeback Player of the Year Award. All of that is what legends are made of, but not necessarily what makes him significant. What he did next does. In the spring of 2011, he left on a journey, a life-changing trek. He and several others were to climb the 19,000-foot Mount Kilimanjaro in Tanzania, Africa to bring awareness to the Wounded Warrior Project. This project was developed by veterans to assist injured servicemen and women of this current generation fighting in the war.

One of the individuals climbing with him was a former United States Marine, Ben Lunak. Ben lost his right leg in Iraq, and on this trip he climbed with a prosthetic limb. As the group reached above 15,000 feet, Ben could no longer go on and asked that Teddy carry the prosthetic limb to the top. As climbers know, every extra ounce is a burden of weight. A struggle. But Teddy carried it not just for Ben, but also for all those wounded soldiers that could never make it to the top. Teddy climbed the remaining 4,000 feet to the top of Mount Kilimanjaro with Ben's prosthetic limb in tow, not for himself, but for others.

Though many may never have known of Teddy Bruschi's football career, they will know of his unselfish efforts to bring awareness to others and to make another's life better. He used his success to position himself for what we all want to ultimately have—a life of significance.

The question is, "Where are you on life's journey, and how are you positioned for living a life of SIGNIFICANCE?" You still have 1440 minutes in each day to get there. Time is ticking.

ANTHONY MEYERS

CHAPTER 11

CARRY AN UMBRELLA

"And when it rains on your parade, look up rather than down. Without the rain, there would be no rainbow."

Gilbert Keith Chesterton
Author

To achieve great things means that you will have to overcome many obstacles. One of the most debilitating obstacles could be the need for affirmation from others to validate your achievement and success. Face it, you want your name in lights. You want to be recognized for your hard work, dedication, and contribution to all mankind. Yes, you want to be riding down Fifth Avenue, New York City, in that bright red convertible, enjoying your very own ticker-tape parade. And, no you don't want to hear thunder rumbling in the distance or feel rain begin to fall during your moment. You don't want to have to ask, "Who would rain on my parade?" Sometimes the answer can be everybody.

You have probably had that moment when you believe that something you have done is worthy of acknowledgment. It is then that you begin to promote yourself. Say you have friends over for a BBQ, and as you take the steaks off the grill and place them on the table, you begin to look for positive feedback. You tune your ears to people eating but you don't hear words that bring you the affirmation you are looking for.

Then, as you are about to erupt, you ask the question, "How does it taste?" You want them to say that it is the best steak they have ever had. What is it that causes you to push questions on people until you get the response you are looking for?

As I mentioned in a previous chapter, you must be prepared that not everybody is going to be one of your fans. There are going to be times that their efforts will be to diminish, demean and demoralize all that you do. They will never give you credit for anything that you do. The mere parting of their lips to tell you something encouraging about what you do would be a complete impossibility.

But let's face it, you want the applause and support of some of the most unlikely people. You want to prove your worth to people who don't care for your success. You may try hard to impress the teacher that said you would fail, that significant other who left you too early, even the former friends who betrayed you. You still look for something from them. I have seen many who have spent a lifetime wanting to impress a parent who has long since left or more detrimental, has died. They hope to prove that they are better than what those people thought.

I know I said it before, but I'll say it again because it's vital. If you are to truly be successful on any level, you must develop a mentality of ignoring your critics and detractors. They are only there to make you hesitate and doubt yourself. Wake up each morning with a plan to be the best you can for that day. Use the 1440 in such a way that there is no room for those types of people to interfere, and if they do squeeze their way into your day, minimize their negative affect.

I have on many occasions been at the end of a particularly contentious meeting or just a crazy day and commented, "This was a good day." Some will say, "After all of this, how can you say it was a good day?" or "Why do you look so cheerful, you should be looking sad." My focus is larger than what just happened, bigger than the current moment. Even though I have not won the battle for the day, the war is not lost.

Even on those so-called bad days, try to use them as fuel and resources for the next battle. Some losses are meant as a training tool for your success, and you need to count them as wins. The time will come when you have to use that experience and will see how valuable it was. Let's face it, your goal is to end the day with more wins than losses. Then you can look back and cheer yourself and walk in your own parade. No umbrella needed.

CHAPTER 12

THE F-WORD

*"The reason birds can fly and we can't is
simply that they have perfect faith, for to have
faith is to have wings."*

James M. Barrie
Scottish author and dramatist

It would be an injustice if I completed this book without explaining the power behind my words. You might assume that if you say or do the right things then good things will automatically come to you. I have seen individuals that look like they have it all, and it seems that whenever they speak or touch anything, they seem to get their heart's desire. I wish that it was always the case.

You have a path that you must discover in order to begin your journey. That journey often comes with difficult detours, adverse situations, and parts that can't be explained. It is at these junctures of life when good words fall on the deaf ears of life and what appears to be positive intentions can sometimes fail. What then do you say? Do? Think? You may decide to revert to old glory or convince yourself that things aren't that bad. But, if you live long enough, hard times do come and you have to eventually face them.

The question you may ask yourself is how are you going to deal with it? What thing will you use to turn the pain off? What is the mechanism that will bring the joy back again or at least make you forget? Looking for a way of escape is the order of the day. But no matter how you try, whatever the effort, there is no way around, over or under. You must go through it. I wish sometimes that I could get a hall pass or a stunt double to stand in for me when times get rough. But that isn't the case.

It gets so dramatic at times; all you can do is use the F-word. I know it's not always proper to use, and many that hear it become offended. But at this point in my life, I really don't care. I'm offended that so many people are concerned that through honest and sincere means success can be developed and maintained using the F-word.

Now don't get it twisted. I'm not reverting back to a time in my life when the f-word (lower case) was truly something very carnal and unforgiving. I have grown and now understand that the power of it all is not mine. My F-word is faith. Yes, faith! My faith has been the anchor in all things of my life. It is the glue that keeps me sane in insane situations.

I know that many may not see this as a valuable asset, but it is the true X factor in all I do. There was a time I would go into major situations with a level of heightened anxiety that would disrupt all that needed to be accomplished. Or, I would even become extremely agitated over many situations, which would prevent me from developing the best teams, or making the best decisions.

Over time, my Christian faith has truly given me a sense of peace and focus for my life and all I do. There is not a moment that goes by that I feel out of control or dismayed. When others are raging, I have an anchor that allows me to remain calm. When others are losing hope and looking for the sky to fall, I'm moving forward like in the HOV lane during a traffic jam. Granted, I do have my moments, as we all do, but those moments don't have a debilitating grip on me with a detrimental effect.

During the near-total financial collapse in 2007, there were those around me that feared the worst. Those were going to be the final days, and all was lost. In a meeting one day, a colleague wanted to know why I wasn't concerned. All at the table turned and all eyes were now on me.

I began to tell them that when the economic upheaval began no one called, emailed, or texted me to ask if I wanted to participate. CNN, FOX, and all the news stations said that in mere hours life would never be the same again with financial doom and total societal ruin. I told them that I prayed about it, put it in God's hands, and was going to have peace. I chose not to participate in life's drama, not to be overly concerned, and to stay on course.

I believe that God has a defined plan for my life, and yours a well. Temporary situations can't stop that plan. Yes, temporary as in until the next news cycle or hurricane, tornado, tsunami, mass shooting, or serial killer strikes again. I stopped worrying some time ago and keep my faith in the plan for my life. No, I don't have all the answers, but I do know that my future is bright and my days filled with hope. I'm on a mission for purpose and fulfillment.

It is this, my faith, which always has control so that I don't become overwhelmed with life and what others want it to be. In the Bible, the apostle Paul wrote in his letter to the Philippian Church, "...I have learned to be content whatever the circumstances."[13] That's how I live and keep my trust, peace, hope, and, most importantly, my faith.

Disasters are going to come. There will be the death of a loved one far too soon, a relationship emotionally disrupted, a child gone astray, or a business or a personal deal gone badly. The moment that it happens you will feel that all is lost. All your attention will be focused on what happened, how you feel about it, and who to blame. Anger and frustration will fuel the day. The true question is: what will you be willing to do? This is the time where your decisions will be crucial and may be life-changing.

There are but two ways to handle what has and is happening. You have the choice to either react or respond in faith. To react is to be led by the swift and powerful wind of your emotions. When you react, you will vacillate between many emotions and make decisions in a blurred frenzy that may create regrettable moments for a later date. Reactions, both verbal and physical, are far too often the extreme polar opposite of what your true intentions are.

I have learned that words spoken in anger, fear, or frustration may feel liberating and justified as you spew them out but are a harsh reality of what you will have to live with in the future. There are some things that we react to that the mere word and gestures of "I'm sorry" will never fix. So, then what? What do you do when all is unraveling and falling at your feet?

I remember several years ago I was participating in a softball game. My wife and two daughters were on their way to watch the game. As the game began there was a screeching thud in the distance, but I was completely focused on the game and didn't pay attention to the sound.

Moments later I heard my name over the PA system. As I left the field to go to the scorer's booth, I was told that the distant sound I heard was my wife's car in an accident across the street. In a mad dash, I ran from the field to the street. By this time emergency vehicles were arriving, and all I encountered was chaos. Glass was scattered in the street, and two cars were twisted in the center. This was not what I had planned for the day. I had the career, the wife, kids, house, and even the dogs. Everything was just perfect.

Running on broken glass, I saw my wife emerging from the car, face bloodied, eyes filled with terror. Some woman whom I still do not know, was holding my youngest daughter as she cried. My oldest was in the backseat, EMT's attending to her. Her head smashed off the rear passenger window, swelling her face and head, and she slid in and out of consciousness. On the way to the hospital, I went into "fix it" mode. I was reacting to the situation, but as I arrived and walked through the emergency room doors, I realized that I could not fix this.

My wife had a swollen face, bloodied nose, and was very sore but no major injuries. My youngest had bruises on her shoulder where the seatbelt pulled, but no major injuries. My oldest, six at the time, was being attended to by five or six doctors. They asked me to wait outside as they worked, but that wasn't going to happen. I didn't move. As her face and head continued to swell, doctors became very concerned and sent her to get an MRI.

Now all I could do was wait. I felt helpless. I discovered that I wanted to react, but I could only react by trying to fix things, but fixing this was not an option afforded to me. This was completely out of my hands. It was during that slow walk as they wheeled my daughter to the MRI that I had to come to grips with the reality that this situation was going to take more than me. This was truly going to be a test of my faith. Did I have enough faith that God would or could intervene and do all that I could not? We all face times like this where we have to make a choice: believe or not. I chose to believe. I chose to respond by clinging to my faith, and by not reacting, trying to be in control.

Those minutes of my 1440 that day were moving too slowly for my comfort, but I waited rather impatiently for the results. The doctors came back about an hour later and were very surprised. There was something they could not understand. She did not have any brain damage; her injury was only limited to soft tissue. They said there would be a large bruise and swelling on her forehead, eye, and cheek area.

After a few hours, we were allowed to go home. I got everyone settled and in bed, and all was quiet. I was relieved. It was all over now, or so I thought. In the middle of the night, my daughter came in and said, "Daddy, help; my stomach hurts." A huge bruise had formed across her stomach, and there was swelling.

In a frantic dash, I drove back to the hospital. They looked at us and said, "What happened?" They too thought everything would be well. The pain and bruising caused them great distress. Another MRI was ordered that revealed some internal bleeding into her stomach. They said that the bleeding may stop, but if not, surgery was the next step. The doctor said that we should wait and watch her overnight to see if the situation would correct itself. If not, she would have surgery in the morning.

This was not the time to react. I needed to respond. My reactions would have been fear, frustration, and helplessness. Those just wouldn't suffice. My response was to exercise my faith, but I had questions. What do I do? What do I say?

As she lay in bed, I sat in a chair nearby and prayed. The one thing that I had not done throughout this ordeal was to take a moment to pause and let God take over. Once I did, I fell asleep in my hospital chair. I was awakened a few hours later by my daughter saying, "I feel better; I'm ready to go home."

Just then, the nurse entered and said that it was time for another scan of her abdomen. After the scan, the doctors said that all was well and we could go home. It took me some years later to fully realize that if I put it all in God's hands, He would take care of it. All of my influence and direction would do little to affect the situation. It wasn't until I truly sat back and let my faith take over and let God intervene.

Now granted, I still have moments where I think I can handle all of my situations, but the more I try, the more I realize that it always takes more than just me. I realize that to get into an argument with God about how I think things should go is to fight in futility. I am not going to win. That's when I have to take a back seat and let faith take over, the faith that truly passes all understanding. Many people will not understand or even want to consider that faith can carry you through any situation. The situation at the hospital was one of those defining moments that tested and developed my faith.

It has been and continues to be one of the things I work on daily. I can't control all that will happen every day, but I can control whether I react or respond in faith. Ultimately, it comes down to how I exercise my faith. What will my response be? My first step is often to pray and look to a Bible scripture to guide me in prayer.

For instance, Jeremiah 29:11 says, "For I know the thoughts that I think toward you, saith the Lord, thoughts of peace, and not of evil, to give you an expected end." [14] Because of my faith, I know that any bad situation is not the end, and peace will ultimately be the order of the day. This has been the challenge of my faith. Will I rely on my ability to react and fix things as I have done in the past, or will I respond by exercising my faith and allowing God to take over?

The humbling of self and the grace of God is what got me through that car wreck and many other moments. I can look back now and see God's hand in so many pivotal points in my life. My wife of over twenty years and two daughters who are now college students have little memory of that fateful day. They have little recollection of one of the most defining moments that changed my life and deepened my faith.

Right at this moment I want to encourage you. If you have read this far, then you should understand the value of each and every minute. You're probably trying to figure out then, how you maximize those minutes. How do you reorganize your life to do all the things that you've read in this book? I would be disingenuous by told you it was easy, because it's not. But it is doable, and you can do it. The same way I did and continue to do, one minute at a time, then one hour at a time, then one day at a time. Don't over complicate it with too many distractions, unrealistic goals or distracting people. Every minute is yours, own them, respect them and use them wisely. But by all measure, protect your minutes, because they are all you have in this life.

"This is the day that the Lord has made; [**all 1440 minutes of it**] let us rejoice and be glad in it."
–Psalm 118:24[15]

NEXT STEPS – THE 10'S

If you're going to maximize every minute of every day, it's more than just thinking about things, it is really doing them. So, these are your next steps. I called them the 10's. They are items that should offer you dynamic and unique experiences and perspectives of life. They are all well worth the time you spend doing them. And you should do as many of these as possible. From albums to listen to and museums to explore the definitive times of history. Life-changing places to see and books to read. It's capped off with 10 things that you must do; or at least try.

Don't get stuck where you are. Don't settle for second-best and don't let anyone tell you that you can't spend your time doing what you need to fulfill your dreams. Enjoy your time and live each moment out well. Each minute is yours.

<u>TOP 10 ALBUMS</u>

- **Marvin Gaye** - 'What's Going On'
- **Michael Jackson** – 'Off the Wall'
- **U2** - 'The Joshua Tree'
- **Stevie Wonder -** 'Songs in the Key of Life'
- **The Beatles** - 'Abbey Road'
- **Nirvana** - 'Nevermind'
- **Fleetwood Mac** - 'Rumours'
- **Prince and the Revolution** - 'Purple Rain'
- **Miles Davis** - 'Kind of Blue'
- **Lauryn Hill** - 'The Miseducation of Lauryn Hill'

TOP 10 MUSEUMS

- **Metropolitan Museum of Art** – NYC
- **Millicent Rogers Museum** - Taos, NM
- **Kigali Genocide Memorial** - Rwanda
- **National 9/11 Memorial & Museum** – NYC
- **National Museum of African American History and Culture** - Washington DC
- **US Holocaust Museum – Wash, DC**
- **Getty Center** – Los Angeles, Calif.
- **National Museum of the American Indian** - Washington, DC
- **National Civil Rights Museum** - Memphis, Tennessee
- **American Museum of Natural History** – NYC

TOP 10 PLACES TO VISIT

- **Times Square** - New York
- **Victoria Falls** - Victoria Falls, Zimbabwe
- **The Western Wall** - Jerusalem, Israel
- **Stonehenge** - Wiltshire, England
- **Great Wall of China** - China
- **Berlin Wall** - East Side Gallery, Berlin
- **Niagara Falls** - New York and Ontario, Canada
- **Mount Kilimanjaro** - Tanzania
- **Golden Gate Bridge** - San Francisco
- **Taj Mahal** - Agra, India

<u>MY TOP 10 BOOKS TO READ</u>

- **The Lion, the Witch, and the Wardrobe** - C.S. Lewis
- **The Color Purple** - Alice Walker
- **To Kill a Mockingbird** - Harper Lee
- **A Tale of Two Cities** - Charles Dickens
- **The Autobiography of Malcolm X** - As Told to Alex Haley
- **Outliers** – Malcolm Gladwell
- **The Lord of the Rings** - J.R.R. Tolkien
- **Roots** – Alex Haley
- **How to Win Friends & Influence People** - Dale Carnegie
- **Purple Cow** - Seth Godin

Bonus Books:
- **Thrusting for Living Water** – Michael J. Mantel
- **Never Settle** – Greg Holder
- **Leadership by The Good Book** – Dave Steward/Brandon Mann
- **In Awe** – John O'Leary
- **Maximize the Moment** – T. D. Jakes

TOP 10 THINGS TO DO

- Volunteer at an Orphanage
- Watch changing of the guard at the Tomb of the Unknown Soldier
- New Years Eve at Times Square
- Participate in a Japanese Tea Ceremony
- Get a Tattoo
- Have a conversation with a Maasai Warrior in Tanzania
- Sit in the Devil's Pool (look it up)
- Wear a hat at the Kentucky Derby
- Learn to Forgive
- Say "I'm Sorry"

Footnotes

1   JOHN F. KENNEDY, "ADDRESS AT RICE UNIVERSITY,"
(SPEECH, HOUSTON, TX, SEPTEMBER 12, 1962), JOHN F. KENNEDY
PRESIDENTIAL LIBRARY AND MUSEUM,
HTTPS://WWW.JFKLIBRARY.ORG/.
2   ELIZABETH HOWELL, "APOLLO 1: A FATAL FIRE," 2017,
SPACE.COM, HTTPS://WWW.SPACE.COM/17338-APOLLO-1.HTML
3   "APOLLO 11 MOON LANDING TIMELINE: FROM LIFTOFF TO
SPLASHDOWN," History.com, https://www.history.com/news/apollo-
11-moon-landing-timeline
4   MARC LEVY, "ET SI C'ÉTAIT VRAI..., VOUS REVOIR, ÉDITION
COMPLÈTE 2 EN 1" (1999). (THIS MIGHT BE AN ANONYMOUS QUOTE BUT
JUST LISTED IN THIS BOOK – I HAVE NOT BEEN ABLE TO VERIFY)
5   CHARLTON T. LEWIS AND CHARLES SHORT, "A LATIN
DICTIONARY," (OXFORD: CLARENDON PRESS, 1879).
6   G. R. WATSON, "THE ROMAN SOLDIER," (ITHACA: CORNELL
UNIVERSITY PRESS, 1969).
7   ASSOCIATED PRESS, "U.S. 400-METER RELAY TEAMS DOOMED
BY FLUBBED HANDOFFS, FAIL TO QUALIFY," AUGUST 21, 2008,
HTTPS://WWW.ESPN.COM/OLYMPICS/SUMMER08/TRACKANDFIELD/NE
WS/STORY?ID=3545991.
8   RUDYARD KIPLING, "REWARDS AND FAIRIES," 1910.
9   "AFTERMATH." "MERRIAM-WEBSTER.COM DICTIONARY,"
HTTPS://WWW.MERRIAM-WEBSTER.COM/DICTIONARY/AFTERMATH.
ACCESSED 11 AUG. 2021.
10   AARON RALSTON, "BETWEEN A ROCK AND A HARD PLACE,"
(ATRIA BOOKS, 2004).
11   DAVE RAMSEY, "THE DAVE RAMSEY SHOW," NEWSTALK 550
KTSA (SAN ANTONIO, TX, SEPTEMBER 3, 2012).
12   GENERAL MOTORS, "GMC HONORS WOUNDED WARRIOR
PROJECT AT ESPY AWARDS, SPONSORSHIP CELEBRATES NEVER SAY
NEVER EFFORTS OF U.S. SERVICE MEMBERS, NFL GREATS," (ESPN
AWARDS CEREMONY, LOS ANGELES, CA, JULY 14, 2011).
13   PHILIPPIANS 4:11, NEW INTERNATIONAL VERSION.
14   JEREMIAH 29:11, KING JAMES VERSION.
15   PSALM 118:24, ENGLISH STANDARD VERSION.

ABOUT THE AUTHOR

Thought Innovator, Purpose Strategist & Social Entrepreneur

Anthony Meyers is a dynamic voice for this modern-day society. As a speaker, audiences will remember Anthony's potent blend of a dynamic message, personal focus, and humor. He has the unique ability to find the exact words to deliver compelling, life-changing messages. He is a commanding presence and sparks revitalization. His words are full of substance and delivered with a dramatic, vibrant style. As an executive coach, he motivates individuals to maximize their opportunities to their fullest potential.

"I embrace the opportunity to develop, mentor, and motivate individuals into recognizing their inherent abilities, then utilizing those abilities to produce an empowering, purposeful life."

Anthony

www.anthonymeyers.com

Made in the USA
Coppell, TX
14 February 2022

73572371R00079